Wearable Vintage Fashion

Vivays Publishing

Published by Vivays Publishing Ltd
www.vivays-publishing.com

A catalogue record for this book is available from the
British Library

ISBN 978-1-908126-27-6

Publishing Director: Lee Ripley
Design: Struktur Design
Printed in China

Wearable Vintage Fashion

Jo Waterhouse & Clare Bridge

Vivays Publishing

1920s

1930s

1940s

1950s

1960s

1970s

1980s

Vintage Street Style

8

26

44

62

82

104

126

146

Introduction

Our lifelong passion for vintage fashion is all very useful in our heads but colourful pictures, step by step demos, even dressing ourselves up are helpful tools for aiding others who are dipping their toe into the world of retro.

At Second Hand Rose, the vintage boutique we run in Worcester UK, we've found that wordy reference books with few pictures aren't very inspirational when trying to assist our customers. We compiled this book to fill that gap on the bookshelf. Gorgeous pictures of Dior and Co. make us drool, but this book will guide you through affordable, collectible and wearable items that you can own too, whatever your budget.

Let us be your tour guides through the fashion eras, using our knowledge gained from working amongst vintage on a daily basis. We're poking through the wardrobes of ordinary people from the 1920s to the 1980s and these clothes carry with them their own social and personal history. Thanks to shops like ours, these garments then go on to be worn again by a new generation of vintage and fashion lovers.

Contemporary fashion designers are inspired by the designs of the past and by studying vintage clothes you'll see how certain designs, shapes and styles are timeless classics, repeated again and again by designers throughout the decades. We find it really interesting to see how designs are recycled through the eras and how cyclical the fashion industry is. For instance, had you noticed before that many of the 70s key looks were in fact inspired by 30s fashion? Or how the big shouldered, power-blouses of the 80s are very reminiscent of the shoulder shapes and blouses of the 40s? We'll point these out as we take you through the decades. It's useful to know, as having a bit of fashion history knowledge is great when you need to recreate the look of a specific era, but you haven't got the authentic items to hand.

We've focused on women's wear in this book, it would have to be a very big book indeed if we were to cover both sexes in the same amount of detail, and being girls we can't help but be more interested in women's fashion and clothing!

We haven't tried to create an encyclopedia of vintage fashion, and haven't included every single style and trend from each decade. Instead this is our selection of key pieces and looks from Western fashion over the years. We've included as much as we can, looking at day and evening outfits for each decade and including a host of accessories.

At Second Hand Rose, part of the job includes dressing people for a specific occasion, be it a party, a vintage festival, re-enactment, or as we've done on occasion, for film, TV and fashion shows. This often requires a bit of creativity and ingenuity. People may want to look like a 40s film siren but don't have the budget for an original 40s gown, or can't fit into their favourite period piece (that's usually the case for us, damn those skinny gals of yesteryear!) but still want to look the part. Here's where we step in

and use that fashion history expertise to recreate and sometimes 'cheat' an authentic looking outfit with non-authentic pieces from other eras, sometimes using modern elements.

In the 'Get the Look' section we've used personal photographs from family and friends alongside outfits and items of period clothing. We thought this was a great way of showing some of the everyday fashions in context and how to recreate their look. Looking at photos of real women in real situations wearing their own clothes is the ultimate way to learn about fashion history and be inspired by wardrobes of the past. Some of the vintage pieces in this book are our own personal treasures, from our own collections, inherited or borrowed from our mothers and grandmothers, so it seemed fitting to include some of their photographs here. Vintage fashion is often steeped in personal history and nostalgia, and that's often its appeal, seeing items we remember from our childhoods or in family albums.

In the 'Icon' sections, we've chosen characters or actresses from films: someone who encapsulates the look of that particular era and who everyone will recognise. We got stuck in and took turns dressing up to recreate the 'Icon' looks for each decade, just to show how easy it is (not to mention how much fun!) to "transform" yourself into your favourite movie star or imitate a period costume in a few short steps. We know we're far from the doppelgangers of Monroe or Fawcett, but by picking out the key elements to an iconic style, donning a wig, and a trowel or two of extra make up, and most importantly getting into the spirit of it, we've recreated looks that could hold their own at any party! Being able to recreate an outfit without using an ill-fitting, off-the-peg costume, that other people could be wearing, is a handy skill to have!

The 'Look Books' at the end of each decade section intend to provide more inspiration for collecting, buying or wearing vintage. We look at day and evening wear for each era, and group together authentic garments and accessories typical of the decade, or more modern items that represent the style of that decade. We will tell you when we use an item that isn't original.

Accessories are very important. They are the key to completing any look, whether an entirely authentic period one or just for fun. It can be the difference between looking a 'little bit vintage' and nailing a specific era look. When recreating an era look, particularly from the 20s to the 50s, accessorising really finishes an outfit and gives it an overall authentic touch, even if the individual items themselves aren't.

When selecting the clothing we wanted to include in the book we focused on items that encapsulate each particular decade, and look unmistakably 'that decade'. This is tricky as fashions and styles continue through the decades, blurring into one another. A great example of this is the classic 1950s full skirted, nipped-in waist look. Most people associate this look with the 50s, but it was a style launched by Dior in 1947 and commonly known as the 'New Look'. It

goes to show how a range launched at the end of the 40s then went on to influence the following decade by trickling down to popular culture through mass production from its haute couture perch.

People's experience of fashion can also differ depending on where you are in your country and the world. For instance during the 60s, the revolution in fashion happening in so-called 'Swinging London', wasn't necessarily happening on the High Streets of provincial towns further up and down the country, the change was more gradual for different areas and people, with some development in style taking much longer, years in fact, to filter through. We've often heard people exclaim indignantly in the shop "I didn't wear that in the 60s!" No madam, you didn't but somebody somewhere certainly did! That's why it's important in this book to generalise to some extent, and show garments and looks that are more universally synonymous with each era, and therefore capture aspects of each decade for everyone.

You'll notice in the 20s and 30s sections in particular, that we've included a few more expensive items, for instance, the flapper dresses and a fabulous velvet cape. These obviously aren't the kind of garments someone would have worn to pop to the shops in or to hang out the washing. Yet they are important to fashion history and in some cases such unusual items and such a find, that we wanted to share them. We do realise they don't quite fit into the everyday theme, however they do show the different kinds of vintage pieces out there to be collected, and these pieces can still be wearable today, albeit for a special occasion. Sometimes when you can afford to, it's worth spending a little bit extra on something truly unique, as these special items rarely come along again. If you care for special buys like these, they will not only last a lifetime, but also increase in value.

The last section of the book really celebrates the idea of wearable vintage clothing. We took submissions from vintage enthusiasts across the globe, many vintage fashion bloggers themselves, in order to document how people are wearing vintage clothing today. These might be fashion lovers who enjoy mixing and matching classic vintage pieces and accessories into their modern, daily wardrobe, or individuals so immersed in a particular era that they 'live' it everyday. When we came across people who love one era's fashion above all others, we've picked their brains about their collections, and inspirations, and asked them for any advice they can pass on to others. It's been fantastic seeing all these snazzily dressed vintage lovers from all over the world. Our many thanks and appreciation goes out to everyone who contributed to this part of the book.

When you love vintage fashion as much as we do, it seemed impossible to imagine having to leave out even one pair of gloves or one of our favourite 50s cotton dresses but we had to be sensible! Although the majority of the items you see in the book are from Second Hand Rose, we are also indebted to several people for filling any gaps we had. There is a complete list of thank yous and acknowledgements at the back of the book, please do have a read through and see where we were able to source some of these wonderful vintage items.

We've really enjoyed putting this book together and have laughed heartily whilst playing dress up. Now it's your turn!

Jo & Clare
www.secondhandroseworcester.co.uk

1920s

The women's Suffrage movement of the early 1900s encouraged the new generation of liberated, young women to cast off their corsets, shake off the stuffy formality of their parents' Edwardian era and embrace life after the tragedy and uncertainty of the war years.

Social, political and economic changes following the First World War were the reasons for significant transformations in attitudes and style, and it could be argued that the 1920s witnessed the first ever youth movement. It was the era of Art Deco which dominated all aspects of design including fashion and jewellery. Designers indulged in the freedom of colour and new, modernist shapes and patterns.

Original 20s and 30s fashions are getting much harder to find, and items from this era in mint condition are no longer affordable. Good quality, genuine garments from the 20s and 30s are likely to set you back well over £100 and the rest are likely to be well worn and resemble rags!

That's not to say you still can't get lucky. Twenties items are very collectible and some accessories from this period are still affordable, so they're a good place to start if you want to recreate the look of this era. Even if you can't get the original pieces, you'll soon be able to spot modern equivalents by getting to know the groundbreaking designs of these years.

Young women were fed up of being trussed up in uncomfortable corsets, and long, heavy skirts; clothing that was previously neck to ankle and all about covering up, became simpler and looser.

When you're looking to find original 20s designs, look for drop waists, and dresses from 1925 generally had hemlines on or just below the knee. These were the shortest skirts ever seen and destined to shock and appall the older generation and there were even movements to outlaw them! Showing a bit of flesh, hanging loose, these girls were carefree without their corsets.

It was a revolutionary time for women's fashion but it didn't happen overnight, it began slowly and as with most innovations in fashion, started with high-end fashion houses pioneering new designs. Coco Chanel is credited with transforming high society women at this time with her use of jersey materials, trousers and abolishing the corset. 'Sportswear' became popular everyday fashion as society seemed to relax its formality and previous conventions after the war. It was the birth of modern fashion as we know it.

Chanel's fashion message of the importance of looking effortlessly stylish soon caught on and by the mid 20s, the lines between social classes blurred for the first time in fashion history. What most people think of as the classic 20s look: the short bobbed hair, knee length dresses and cloches were universal for all ages and social sets. The hats themselves required the shorter bobbed hairdo in order to wear them successfully. The cloche is an easy way to get ahead with a 20s look!

From this new breed of liberated, independent minded women an androgynous fashion trend also transpired, beginning in the upper classes. An even shorter 'Eton crop' hair cut was sported, so named as it resembled a schoolboy's hair cut. Wide legged trousers or 'pyjamas' were worn for leisure, on the beach and for sport. Sportswear gained a wider popularity for all. These 'Bright Young Things' were trendsetters and were well turned out in daring and decadent looks. Celebrity culture hit the headlines and stylish snaps accompanied salacious stories.

The flapper dress is what really epitomizes the 20s and the ethos of the 'Bright Young Things'. The classic flapper evening dress is knee length, sleeveless, with a drop waist, and is usually heavily beaded or sequined. The 20s were heavy on the embellishments for evening wear: ladies were keen to be seen. Evening bags were small and beaded, there were also bead fringes on bags and dresses. Fur was everywhere for coats and trimmings for day and night. Coats would quite often have large fur collars and cuffs and the archetypal style was a wrap over coat fastened with one button, just below the waistline.

Accessories during the 20s were often Art Deco inspired and included trinkets from far flung travels such as hair combs, dress clips, jewellery, day and evening gloves and scarves. A big influence on the era's designs was the exotic.

African, especially Egyptian, and oriental designs were also very popular in fabric patterns and styles. Kimonos and kimono elements such as large, square sleeves appeared on dresses.

20

"Wait a minute,
    you ain't seen anythin' yet"

Daywear

This is a 1920s, printed silk day dress. The front would have a modesty panel beneath the opening which has gathering and button detail. This dress has a drop waist, the key feature of 1920s garments. We've accessorised this dress with original period shoes, that have a shapely heel, an original bag with oriental scene on it. The bag would be carried, tucked under the arm. We've added an original carved, bone bangle. Bangles were a popular accessory that incorporated the decade's exotic influences. The cloche is a 60s reproduction, but the cloche pin is an original 20s piece. Small drop earrings are in keeping with the era, these black glass earrings aren't original but are in the style of those from the 20s.

Flapper Dress

This is a classic, dramatic flapper outfit, using all original items. A flapper dress is generally knee length and sleeveless with a drop waist and usually much embellishment. These dresses were made to dance in, so the shape and construction reflected this: there are often layers, fringes, tassels and beads, all designed to move and sparkle.

Accessories included here are a beaded drawstring evening bag; the style of this particular one was popular before the turn of the century, all kinds of drawstring beaded bags were in vogue during the 20s. These satin, evening shoes with diamante detail, clearly show the curved, 20s style heel. There is also a Deco bracelet with bakelite and diamante segments.

This glamourous evening cape is obviously not an 'every day' item, made from devore velvet, capes were very popular in the 20s.

Top left is an original, delicately beaded, flapper headband. This would have been worn low over the forehead. With her sharp, fringed bob, a flapper in this would have certainly had an air of Cleopatra about her.

Long beads are an essential flapper accessory, this is an original, long, chunky bakelite chain.

Underwear was unrestrictive for the first time in a long time for women in the 20s. Look at this cheeky, hand crocheted bra, not much support here!

More sparkles to catch the light, with this very Deco-style marcasite ring.

Long button-up evening gloves finish this outfit off a treat.

Beaded Bags

Here we have a selection of bags of varying ages.

These bags are still fairly easy to find, more affordable and very collectible. When looking for originals keep an eye out for glass beads, plastic versions are more modern. The beaded drawstring bags were popular from the late 1800s and through the 1920s.

Handles on purses are often a single small strap to slip your hand through, out of sight at the back, as seen here.

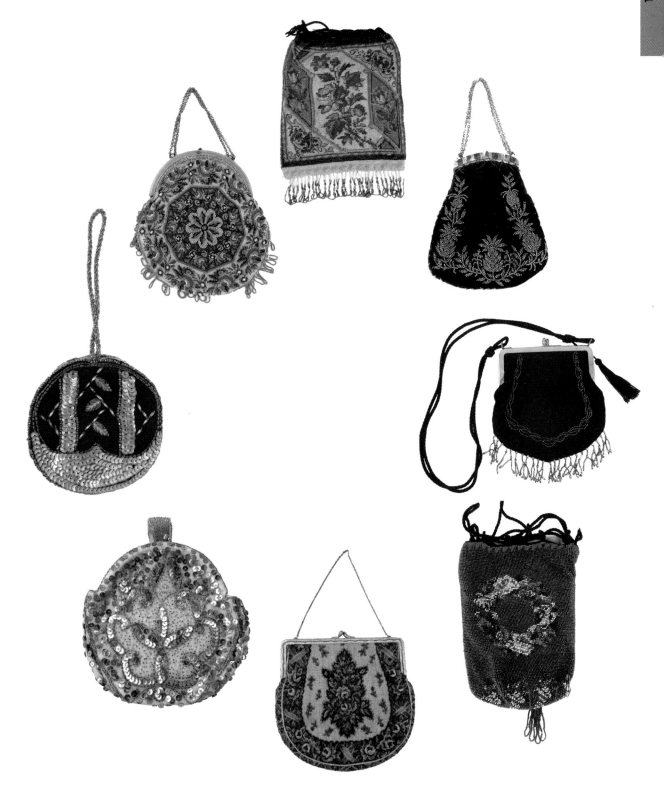

Get the Look

Look at these fabulous photos of typical 20s gals about town. As you can see everyone is wearing a cloche hat. To get a classic 20s look cloches must be worn! The three cloches we've shown on these pages aren't original, they're cloche-styles from the 60s which is a great era to plunder for a 20s look hat.

Looking at the photos, other popular accessories at the time include long beads, gloves and fur stoles, coats and collars. Below is a vintage 20s fox fur. It's undeniable that real fur was a huge part of ladies' wardrobes in the 20s, as you can see. It's a controversial subject, but obviously you could recreate a 20s look just as well with a faux fur stole.

On the mannequin we have a typical 20s, side fastening, knee length coat with a furry collar. Underneath is a reproduction 20s dress.

Shoes typically fastened with buckles, one, two or t-bars are most fashionable, as shown, but it's the shapely heel of a 20s shoe that is most recognisable. Bags tend to be small, hand held clutches. We've used a 70s leather clutch here, that looks the part.

17

Get the Look

The photos (far left) show off some fantastic 20s dresses with much more summery looks. In the summer months, straw cloches would be worn, along with white versions of the classic 20s shoe. This is a lovely example of a hand-embroidered straw cloche. This lovely bit of detailing would set the wearer apart from the crowd.

You can see from the photos that dresses were striped and patterned, with collars and tiers and more beads. In the two dresses we have here, you can see the shapeless style of the 20s designs. Lengths were longer at the start and end of the decade. Ties at the front of dresses were a popular feature, so were scarves, which create a similar effect.

Here's a picture of a young lady, Winnie, in her wonderful scalloped, beaded flapper dress, posing by a pond. The new knee length dresses were scandalous at the time. Our flapper dress here shows the delicate bead work in more detail, and on this particular dress, its daring sheer panel, which would have been worn with a slip. We teamed this dress with some golden satin, two-button shoes and a matching authentic, circular, beaded bag. The 80s produced some fabulous sequinned gowns, some of which definitely emulate the flapper spirit, try these to get this look, especially for a party, as most originals are now too delicate to actually wear.

ICONS

1920s Icon: Louise Brooks

We chose to recreate the look of 20s film star Louise Brooks as her trademark bob epitomises the look of the era. There were lots of images of her to choose from but we went for the easiest way of recreating a look from the 20s using 'look alike' clothing.

Jo is wearing an 80s drop-waist dress with pleating, and a 1970s, fur-lined coat. Both these items are so typical of the era and there are photographs of Ms Brooks wearing a very similar coat. These sorts of coats in the 20s would have had a one-button fastening just under the waist, to recreate this you could just cross the coat over and tie with a ribbon or belt on the hips.

Louise Brooks has been photographed in cloches and headscarves, and we've used a thin, satin scarf, wrapped round the head and tied at the side to create a cross between these two styles. This is also the perfect way of creating the illusion of a 'bob' if you don't actually have one, like Jo here.

Shoe-wise, a modern heeled brogue looks the part with the laces exchanged for ribbon. Other accessories are a cheap, repro set of long pearls, and you could carry a clutch or small beaded bag to complete the look for a party, re-enactment or fancy dress.

Have you ever noticed how ladies in old 20s photographs all looked practically the same? This is all down to how they applied their make up. We've shown in the photo just how easy it is to transform your appearance by applying 20s style make up. The trick is angular brows, dark eyes (lots of eyeliner all round but no 'cats-eye' flicks) but the icing on the cake is the lipstick. That's how ladies dramatically changed their appearance: they'd essentially white out parts of their natural lipline and draw on the popular lip shape of the time: small and pointy, then powder over the rest of the lips. In photographs it isn't always easy to spot, but it's the best way of putting the finishing touches to an authentic looking 20s outfit.

Make-up tips

Long, dark, thin penciled eyebrows, take the line further than where they naturally end.

Lots of dark matt eyeshadow, all over the eyelid and socket, take it into the inner corner of the eye for a dramatic look, make sure you blend well.

Use concealer to blank out your natural lip line and use a dark plummy red or purple. Create a smaller upper lip with exaggerated, pointy cupids bow shape.

Apply your foundation after doing your eye make-up as it can be messy! A pale face was in vogue.

1920s

Look Book / Daywear

Here we have a selection of daywear from the 20s, showing more variety in designs, details and styles.

Brown wool day dress with low V-neck. This dress had an unusual dressmaker and size label inside, as well as a a lovely, gold coloured and diamante belt buckle. Dresses like this would have been worn over a slip such as the black and white one alongside it, which create a 'modesty panel' at the front.

Crocheted skull cap, these were worn in bed or sometimes out in a motorcar to keep your flapper bob neat.

Suede Deco, triangular shaped handbag.

Brass Deco lady with wolf hound, a popular dog of the era.

Glass cameo, a classic piece of jewellery popular through many decades.

Lime green silk 'step in' slip. These are all in one slips that you literally had to step into, and were a revolutionary new style of underwear at the time.

Pink silk dress with archetypal drop waist, square neckline and pleated skirt.

Gold metal bird, coloured foil design.

The black lace-up boots from the 1990s, make a perfect 20s-looking lace-up.

Embroidered silk dress, European made. A good example of the intricate decoration/ embellishment of the era.

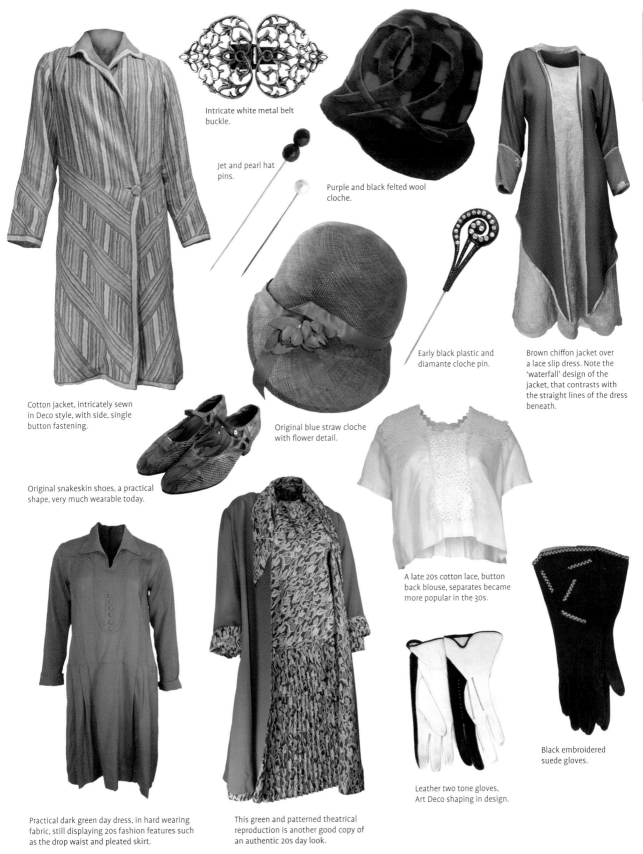

Intricate white metal belt buckle.

Jet and pearl hat pins.

Purple and black felted wool cloche.

Early black plastic and diamante cloche pin.

Brown chiffon jacket over a lace slip dress. Note the 'waterfall' design of the jacket, that contrasts with the straight lines of the dress beneath.

Cotton jacket, intricately sewn in Deco style, with side, single button fastening.

Original blue straw cloche with flower detail.

Original snakeskin shoes, a practical shape, very much wearable today.

A late 20s cotton lace, button back blouse, separates became more popular in the 30s.

Black embroidered suede gloves.

Leather two tone gloves, Art Deco shaping in design.

Practical dark green day dress, in hard wearing fabric, still displaying 20s fashion features such as the drop waist and pleated skirt.

This green and patterned theatrical reproduction is another good copy of an authentic 20s day look.

Look Book / Eveningwear

Evening wear of the 20s for the affluent was luxurious, glamourous and sparkling. These items are to inspire a 20s evening look of your own.

Marcasite belt buckle.

Celluloid brooch with dancing couple, a 'snap shot' of the decade's fashion.

Luxurious black velvet, fur collared coat with gold brocade velvet evening gown, with large, gold metal belt buckle.

Early plastic hair comb, with Deco sun burst design. A pre-20's accessory worn in long hair 'up do's' popular before the short bob dominated.

Diamante Deco design brooch.

Blue devore velvet flapper style dress.

Soft orange silk dress with geometric pattern, and matching drop waist belt.

Original satin evening shoes.

Diamante hat pin.

Early plastic, foil-backed dress clips, usually worn either side of a square neckline or on each strap for embellishment.

Long, gold leather gloves.

Soft blue, long, suede gloves with decadent diamante embellishment.

Original silk embroidered kimono style dressing gown, example of exotic/eastern influence.

Black velvet dress with stitched diamante jewels in an exotic style 'necklace' shape.

Marcasite hair pins, pre-20s but still worn throughout the decade.

A modern kimono, a style classic produced throughout the 20th century and perfect to recreate a 20s boudoir look.

A devore velvet evening jacket.

Black suede gloves with diamond pattern.

Diamante and tortoise shell plastic dress clips.

Oriental style, early plastic hair comb.

1930s

In the 1930s hemlines fell as well as the economy with the stock market crash of 1929. From now on hemlines would be seen to reflect the general state of economic affairs. The difficult years for many that followed, finished off the flapper-era and ushered in a more grown-up decade.

The 30s took over the fashion reins from the revolutionary 20s and the explosion of the modern, media age developed women's clothing into new and glamourous never before seen styles. Whereas the 20s were about suppressing a woman's natural shape, the 30s were all about embracing it. Construction of clothing saw great innovations with new, synthetic fabrics and the first commercial use of the zip in clothing manufacture. Despite this, it'd still be rare to find a zip in everyday, handmade dresses of the 30s. Side fastenings using press studs are the most common. The popularization of bias-cut dresses, which gave fabrics more stretch provided clever concepts for fit and drapery.

The 30s have been dubbed the 'golden age' of Hollywood. Every woman looked to the stars of the silver screen for fashion inspiration as well as escapism. The revealing gowns of the starlets were recreated by ordinary girls to make an entrance at the local dance hall. Although hemlines had dropped there were still outrages to be caused: this was the first time that women's clothing was overtly sexy and newly favoured were strappy, backless, figure hugging gowns for evening wear.

In the 30s paid holidays became the law in Britain, so a boom in leisure time, activities and leisure wear followed for the working classes, bringing with it new designs in swim and resort wear, such as the wide legged trouser. It would still be awhile longer, however, before trousers were acceptable everyday wear for women.

Waists returned to the natural waistline during the 30s, and Chanel designed her first classic two-piece suit which was an almighty influence on women's fashion, still dominated by dresses. The most sort after items today from the 30s, are the pretty day dresses in feminine florals, often with bows at the neck and thin belts with bakelite buckles. The best-dressed gals about town would take afternoon tea in these, whether they were homemade by mother or by a well-known dressmaker. The outfit wouldn't be complete without the essential matching accessories of bags, hats and gloves, especially the gauntlet shaped gloves of this period

The ubiquitous cloche was quashed in the 30s, and hats became much more adventurous coming in all shapes and sizes including berets and pillbox hats.

Despite the hard times seen in the 30s, worse was yet to come. Frivolous and flimsy fashions would be replaced with the frugal forties.

"BUT NOW GOD KNOWS,
IN FASHION,
ANYTHING GOES!"

Daywear

Here's a perfect example of a 30s tea dress, one of the key and most popular looks of the decade. Dresses are back to a demure, full length after the shorter skirts of the mid to late 20s. The hat here is reproduction, but hats in the 30s did come in all shapes and sizes and are therefore easier to emulate. All the other items are genuine 30s pieces. The floral dress is made from crepe. We love this gorgeous hand embroidered, handmade bag, with bakelite handles. The beads are also bakelite, an early plastic, popular for jewellery during this decade. There's lots of sophisticated matching colours here with the green carved earrings and matching green suede gloves and shoes.

Another original tea dress, this one has a matching jacket and metal deco belt detail. It's always such a bonus to find a dress with its original belt, these are usually the first things to disappear. We've accessorised this look with white gauntlet gloves, a fashionable shape of the time.

These brown shoes are 1920s but would still have been worn into the next decade, the shape was still fashionable and shoes were made to last. Here's another more extravagantly embroidered handbag, with dark brown bakelite handle.

The hat is a really interesting piece, a knitted beret made from a plasticised material and pinned into place with ribbon detail. After the universal cloche hats of the 20s, hat designs became really inventive.

Leisurewear

Holidays were an important part of life in the 30s. Here we have a selection of original beachwear including: 'beach pyjamas' which were upper class attire designed for sauntering along the coast, or lounging in the sun, possibly whilst wearing this over-sized coolie hat. Modern looking swimwear was quite a new invention in the 30s, they were often black and woollen which wasn't especially practical when wet! This highly patterned, late 30s swimsuit would have belonged to a very fashionable lady. Covering up was also important, and this coral coloured beach jacket with coral and fish embroidered design, was again another highly fashionable piece.

This early plastic seagull brooch is very collectible now. These whimsical novelty brooches grew in popularity through this era.

These are reproduction 30s sunglasses, a classic shape popular throughout the 30s and 40s.

Eveningwear

This is a dramatic evening outfit which has subtle elements that define it as distinctly 1930s. There's the sumptuous sequinned velvet, on a body hugging, strappy, layered dress; the 30s were all about showing off the figure. Note the unusual silver shoes have a much straighter heel than 20s shoes.

We've added faux-marcasite and diamante jewellery to this outfit, faux-marcasite is punched metal rather than individual stones. Marcasite jewellery is still made today, but was first made about 400 years ago. Pieces from the early 20th century are still very affordable and were popular Deco adornments. Many different, intricate designs were reproduced throughout the 20th century making them very collectible pieces.

Get the Look

The 30s are epitomised by the floral tea dress. This style of dress was popular in the next decade too and saw a revival in the 80s. In the 30s they were often made from cotton, or new fangled man made fibres such as rayon or acetate. In the photos there are various styles and designs of dresses, from spotty with frilly, short sleeves to floral with cuff sleeves. To get this look, we've used an 80s floral dress with a perfectly era-friendly lace modesty panel, a style that can be seen in the photos on dresses worn by Winnie and her mother Nellie. The sleeves on this dress could be turned back to create cuffs like Nellie's dress. Crepe, silk, chiffon and some early man-made are the fabrics to look for as far as the 30's are concerned, cutting on the bias was often the technique used to construct a fashionable garment. This dusky pink original 30s dress is made from crepe. It's an example of a plainer day dress, but it has interesting smocking detail.

We've accessorised the summery look on the right with an original 30s straw hat, but an 80s one would also fit. Bags were still mostly handheld or clutches, we've found a later one that's similar to Nellie's, and finishes this outfit off perfectly.

Shoes of this era often still had the 20s heel. Any 'Mary Jane' style shoe worn with ankle socks would look the part. A finishing touch could be a pair of round spectacles like the lady in the deckchair. These original frames are from Dead Men's Spex who specialise in vintage spectacles (details at the back of the book.)

Necklaces worn here are more delicate, but chunky bakelite or other plastic beads would still be worn.

Get the Look

You can just make out the date on this photograph from Blackpool - 1935. This lady is wearing a very popular 30s hat shape. It's a small brimmed, woven hat with ribbon round it. Our original hat here is almost identical, shown from the back it has a gathered ribbon detail. This 30s silk dress has a similar tie neck to the one in the picture. For dresses with front features, wear a short set of pearls or beads like the lady in the photograph.

Separates became very popular in the 30s with blouses, skirts, jumpers and jackets. Here's a lovely 30s blouse with bows at the neck and waist, and slightly puffed sleeves which was a desirable style, as can be seen in the photo on Winnie. You could wear it with a calf length, straight skirt or with white, high waisted, wide leg trousers for a perfect 30s holiday look.

On the upper right we see Winnie and Nellie in their black, woollen swimsuits! Our original 30s swimsuit here is actually a man's, which as you can see, was very similar to women's, no speedos yet! The anchor brooch is another example of the novelty brooches popularised in the 30s, often made as souvenirs, capitalising on the growth of the holiday industry.

On the lower right there is another example of an intricate 30s hat. It's most likely handmade, moulded felt with bow and flower details. This authentic alligator handbag has a very stylish 30s style clasp, and would go nicely with this hat and a 30s or 30s-looking dress to accessorise this period look.

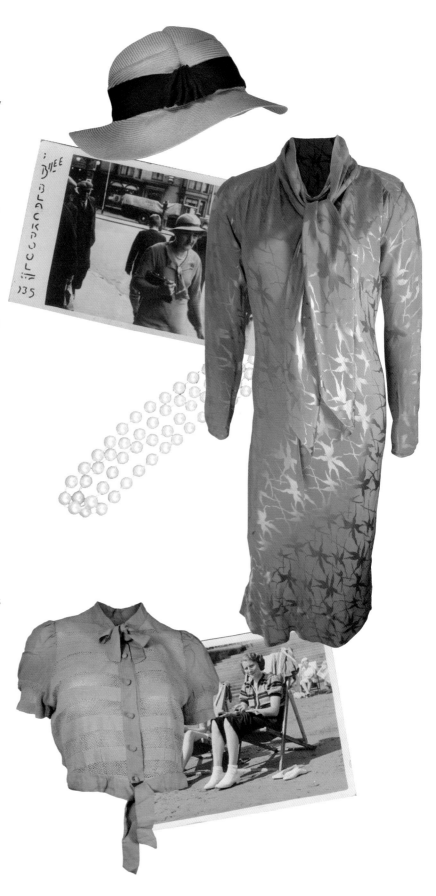

ICONS

1930s Icon – Bonnie Parker

For the 30s iconic look we've recreated the famous outfit from the film Bonnie and Clyde. Released in 1967, it starring the beautiful Faye Dunaway as the notorious and deadly Bonnie Parker. This film apparently single-handedly revived interest in the beret at the time. The outfit from the film is more recognisable and is a much more stylised version of what the real Bonnie Parker would have worn.

To recreate this look Jo's wearing an 80s tweed skirt with box pleats, the length should reach below the knee, a fine knit sweater and a beret. To recreate this look, search for the separates in creams, browns and earth-tones where possible.

The important element in this outfit is the scarf in complementing colours tied loosely in a triangle at the neck, which makes this look instantly recognisable. We've picked some sturdy lace-up shoes similar to those used in the film. You could also wear 'Mary Jane' style, one-strap shoes in place of these, which would still look in keeping.

To further accessorise we've included gloves and a leather clutch bag. You could even get a toy gun to carry as the finishing touch.

As the hair is fairly recognisable from the film, we've used a wig which has come in handy for a few costume changes as you'll see!

We like this look as it's a cheeky alternative costume to the traditional Hollywood glamour that is usually associated with the 1930s.

Thin, over plucked sculpted brows were in, conceal your natural brow shape and add a long thin line over the top, adding extra outer length.

Pale eyelids, extra coats of mascara, no obvious eyeliner or eyeshadow.

Well defined lips with exaggerated rounded 'cupids bow' top lip in red.

A healthy rouged cheek completes the look.

Look Book / Daywear

Here we have some more interesting 30s day pieces. As you can see the natural waistline has started to reappear on most dresses by the start of the decade, and jewellery became quirkier and more inventive.

Butterfly Trembler Brooch, so named as the wings are sprung to tremble with movement.

Sculptural, black felt hat.

Navy and white, wide brimmed straw hat. This is from the 80s but replicates the 30s style.

Lovely cream, late 30s dress with matching spotty belt and scarf, with black bakelite buckle and buttons.

This dark orange dress has ornate detailing to the front, shoulder and sleeves. The belted waist with bakelite buckle accentuates the new womanly silhouette. Dressmaker made clothing was popular and this piece was a fine example of that skill.

Intricate, tooled leather satchel, handbag.

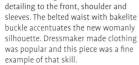

Homemade, original lace blouse with silk panel designed to tuck into a skirt or wide-legged trousers.

White leather gauntlet style gloves.

Carved and painted, early plastic brooches.

Another version of our Bonnie Parker 'icon' look, using more modern pieces. This heavy wool skirt falls below the knee and has side pleats.

Black daisy print crepe bias cut dress.

A later wool beret, but a classic design seen through this decade, and unchanged through the century.

White and navy early 30s leather shoes.

White leather gauntlets with fancy fastening.

Leather snakeskin handbag.

39

Look Book / Daywear

Carved flower brooch, this sort of brooch was popular into the 40s.

Carved novelty dog brooch.

A 30s style hand knit cardigan. A non-original piece, but it would add authenticity to a 30s outfit, as knitting was very popular and in decades to follow. If you're talented in this department original patterns are easy to come by.

Oriental dragon, tooled leather handbag.

This vintage watch has a 30s looking face. Wearing a period watch with an outfit is a really nice touch!

Exotic bird-print silk dress and detail, exotic prints and designs were still prevalent throughout this decade.

Black 'bo peep' style, original 30s hat.

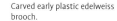

Carved early plastic edelweiss brooch.

Cream and Navy, woven leather t-bar shoes.

A selection of 30s compacts, a lady wouldn't leave home without hers.

'Butterscotch bakelite' belt buckle.

Grey leather gloves.

Tortoise shell hair pin - real tortoise shell was a popular deco material, and longer hair in the 30s meant for more styling.

Great example of a 30s classic: bias cut tea dress, floral print in acetate. Acetate is a manmade fibre that is lightweight and has a sheen like some silks. Man made fabrics became more common with the birth of mass produced garments.

Wonderful vibrant coloured, embroidered handbag with bakelite handles.

Amber and metal bracelet, a later piece but the shape and colouring is right for this era.

Look Book / Eveningwear

30s evening wear was more daring and dazzling than the previous decade, with figure hugging, low-back gowns and more embellishments.

Black and multi-colour, painted acetate blouse.

Red, oriental theme, embroidered satin bag with short chain strap.

Intricately embroidered oriental silk jacket.

Floral, afternoon/evening dress with matching capelet.

Deco metal painted bird brooch.

Geometric patterned crepe evening dress.

Lozenge shaped, rhinestone and faux-marcasite deco brooch.

70s evening maxi dress with the shape and length of a 30s dress, and the chiffon butterfly-style sleeves popular at the time.

Black suede gauntlet with fancy scalloped detailing.

Glass bamboo-shaped shoe clip. You can spot a shoe clip from a dress clip, as it has a more robust fastener.

Small, satin and ribbon work clutch bag with period clasp.

30s peach satin, quilted bed jacket. These aren't popular at all nowadays, but vintage bed jackets can make a fantastic unusual cropped jacket when worn today.

Velvet turban hat with gold embellishments.

Orange and white patterned dress and cape. Note the plunging back and bias cut, design features synonymous with the daring, figure hugging gowns of the 30s.

30s light green satin pyjamas, perfect for luxurious lounging.

RUSSELL & BROMLEY

STYLED by TOBY J

Delicate cream lace evening jacket.

Russell and Bromley Brocade satin and gold leather t-bar shoes. Note the move to a straighter, higher heel.

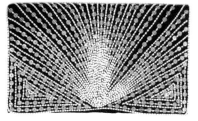

Evening bag with Deco, sunburst beading. This is an early 80s bag, but hand held would accessorise a 30s look perfectly.

Frilly gauntlets.

1940s

The 1940s were dominated by World War II which was a huge influence on the fashion of the time, out of necessity and also respect for the war effort.

Women worked harder than ever, but the 'We Can Do It' and 'Of Course I Can' propaganda of the time meant they also did it with style and pizzazz.

Certain fabrics and materials were scarce and needed for the war so UK clothing was rationed from 1941 until 1949. Clothing coupons were required, limiting the amount of clothing people could buy.

The CC41 (Controlled Commodity 1941) label was introduced by the British Government and put on clothing and other items designed to meet new standards of utility and non-wastefulness. Clothing was streamlined so that there were no unnecessary pockets, buttons or other details. Hemlines rose again in the 40s to just below the knee for daywear, which meant less fabric was needed to make a dress or skirt. Don't be fooled into thinking that this meant style was sacrificed, the Government enlisted the help of amongst others, renowned designers Hardy Amies and Norman Hartnell (dressmaker to the Queen) to create the compact CC41 range to boost morale. So a working woman could hold her head high in 'designer' utility wear.

The CC41 label is always worth looking out for; it can be tucked away in an armpit or pocket seam and can add value to the garment. Clothing and manufacturing labels offer great clues to a garment's age, and became more prominent in the 40s.

The 40s were the decade of women at work and many new styles for women were born from practicality. Everyday clothing took on a practical and patriotic, military look and women's suits resembled uniforms. The 40s were the era for sharp tailoring on a budget. Despite the long lines of jackets, there was always the emphasis on the waistline for a feminine silhouette. Wide lapels and extreme padded shoulders accentuated this. The power-dressing trend of the 80s was influenced by the strong working women of the 40s.

Women literally wore the trousers and were required to work in factories and on the land. Their high-waisted work pants or slacks, had buttons at the side and wearing trousers became more widespread particularly with young women. Jumpsuits were invented in the 40s as Siren or Shelter Suits. They were a warm, all in one suit designed to be worn over clothing and pyjamas in the air raid shelters. They were very practical and had large, handy pockets to carry everything you might need with you.

It was no doubt important for ladies of the 40s to look pretty and presentable at all times. For married or betrothed young women it was seen as a national duty to look their best: they were the pin-ups for their chaps away fighting.

As well as sombre, military coloured garments there were also new, bright colours too. These attempted to counteract the limitations in clothes manufacturing and jolly-up outfits. Women also became adept at cheering up hats and clothes with feathers, felt flowers, or beading. It was however deemed unpatriotic and in bad taste, to be seen to be looking too extravagant with your wardrobe.

It was the era of 'make do and mend' and everyone was encouraged to make the most out of what they already had, particularly in the UK where clothing coupon allowances shrank year by year. Girls became more imaginative, creating new looks from something old, even men's suits were cut up and remade as ladies' outfits. Handmade accessories meant that women were able to change their appearance for relatively little expense. Hats, gloves, bags, scarves and brooches could all be made at home from felt and other materials. Sewing, knitting and crocheting were popular ways to make new items on a budget. Fair Isle knitting patterns were a particularly popular style in 40s Britain for men, women and children, a traditional style that can still be bought today.

Tea or day dresses are a key look from the era, and one that's often replicated by re-enactors and 40s enthusiasts, it's what we get asked to recreate most in the shop. They are usually cotton or rayon shirt-waist, or shirt dresses, in a plain or patterned fabric. The shoulders would be wide, the waist fitted, with a slightly flared skirt ending just below the knee. A similar style can be found in some late 80s and 90s dresses, which work well to recreate this look.

The public's obsession with Hollywood continued as an escape from the realities of war and its aftermath. Women in America were pretty much unaffected by clothing rationing which made them seem more glamourous than their British counterparts and many 40s enthusiasts today prefer to look to the USA for vintage inspiration.

If you were lucky enough to require an evening gown, they were typically floor length and worn with fur or matching caplets or stoles. Fur was still a staple of most women's wardrobes. Embellishments such as beads and sequins weren't rationed or scarce in the 40s, so evening wear would often feature a little sewn-on razzle dazzle.

Hats were a must and very distinctive. There were a variety of hat styles and shapes and many hats were homemade from felt or hand knitted. They were often masculine and military in style and worn further forward and angled down, another nod to the Forces influence.

Headscarves were hugely popular, especially worn as turbans, which were a practical way of keeping your hair clean and tidy during a day in the factory, and were a cost effective alternative to a new hat.

Famous 40s hair-dos such as the Victory Rolls were also born out of a practical need for women to keep their hair out of their eyes and out of factory machinery. This is a perfect example of the practical glamour of the 40s: hair wasn't just scraped back, elaborate new up-dos were invented!

A 40s gal's shoe collection was nothing like it is today. It would be limited to just a few pairs and somewhat unglamourous, sensible day shoes: mid-heels, or masculine flat shoes for factory and land army workers. There were higher heels, platforms shoes and wedges around in the 40s, but these were predominately reserved for stage and screen; practicality was the order of the day.

In 1947 Dior famously revealed his 'New Look' and created a stunning silhouette for women using yards of material for skirts, with a teeny, cinched in waist. The look was shocking for most still experiencing the shortages of war, and seen as wasteful and distasteful by many. It took another several years for this 'new look' to translate to everyday fashion and become a staple look of the next decade.

"KEEP CALM AND CARRY ON LOOKING FABULOUS"

Daywear

This suit has a real military feel. Note the accentuated waist, and square shoulders, as well as the details either side of flap-less pockets. This is a great example of a classic 40s suit.

We've accessorised this outfit with authentic snakeskin shoes and matching bag. The heels of shoes are now wider and sturdier for daywear.

The small woven hat has interesting plastic bow details. Hats were nearly always worn for smart daywear. We've chosen coordinating tan leather gloves to match the bag and shoes. We've included in our 'Look Book' section the type of blouse that would've been worn underneath the suit. A scarf tucked in at the neck is a very smart way to finish the suit off and we've included a carved plastic brooch to be worn on the lapel.

String shopping bags were often crocheted at home and this macramé one is a 70s version, but makes a great substitute. This style resurfaced in the 70s with the craft movement.

It's hard to believe that this dress is original 40s, the colours are so vibrant and the styling still current! This pinky-purple colour crops up a lot of 40s clothing. The austerity of the war years was often counter-balanced with bright, cheerful colours.

These black suede and snakeskin shoes are a fantastic example of an early platform, another style that would be resurrected in the 70s.

Note the exaggerated angles of the hat. It's fairly small and would have been worn towards the front of the head. Angular hats worn in this way are often known as 'tilt hats'.

We've finished this look with some white and purple gloves, white plastic earrings, a feathered bird brooch and a black envelope bag to match the shoes. All items shown here are authentic 40s pieces.

The War Years

Here are some examples of British Wartime wear. The main image is of genuine Women's Land Army, official issue jodhpur trousers, a shirt and Fair Isle knit . You can see the detail from the label inside the trousers. Long, knee high socks would be worn over them, as well as practical boots or shoes, like the pair shown on the opposite page.

The Women's Land Army girls often wore turbans to keep their hair out of the way whilst working, as shown here.

On this page we've included a 70s polyester jumpsuit that is almost a replica of the 40s siren or 'shelter suit'. It was the first jumpsuit, designed to be pulled on quickly during an air raid, in order to keep warm in the shelter.

Clothing in the 40s often bore the utility label. The CC stood for 'Controlled Commodity' and 41 was the year it was introduced, designed to reduce waste and scale back the clothing industry to support the war effort.

The green uniform here is an original WVS - Women's Voluntary Service - uniform and jacket.

On these pages there's a mixed selection of war time brooches, some with patriotic subject matter. The horseshoe and lozenge shaped brooches are made from sealing wax. These and the spitfire brooches are most likely examples of 'trench art jewellery' when a decorative piece was made by a soldier during the war to send back to his loved one.

The wire brooches are fantastic examples of 'make do and mend' using a curtain ring and electrical wire and buttons to create these pretty adornments.

Get the Look

These family photos are a great resource to see what real ladies of the 40s wore and to take inspiration from their wardrobes.

We are using genuine 40s items alongside more modern copycat pieces to recreate these outfits from the past.

To the right is a smart navy, full length coat. Key features are the wide shoulders and lapels, as also seen on the photo.

Scarves, gloves, hats and brooches all finished off an outdoor look.

Original 40s hats like the one below and seen in Charles & Pearl's wedding photo, can be hard to come by. You can easily recreate the look of a 40s hat by reshaping and angling down, a brimmed felt hat. You can also wear a beret, a popular choice as see on the photo above of a gaggle of 40s gals.

We have put together a smart day look, entirely out of 80s pieces, using a tweed skirt, embroidered blouse and a checked, 3 button jacket. An 80s felt hat at the right angle gives off the 40s look to a tee. In the photo Doreen is wearing a similar outfit, with the addition of some 40s round sunglasses, just like the original pair shown here.

Top right we have an original 40s day dress like the one Betty and friend are wearing in the photo. The sharp shoulder, narrow waist and flared skirt are the key features of this look.

Get the Look

These ladies in the photos are making the most of a 40s summer, in jolly patterned tea dresses. The bright colours were a contrast to the drudgery of the war years, and a great way to keep cool and remain stylish. The turquoise patterned dress here is an original 40s number, while the red and green patterned dress is an 80s lookalike, notice the similarities in shape and cut?

This is an authentic 40s suit, and it's undoubtedly an iconic look of the era. This time there's a pleated skirt, but the jacket still clearly shows the square shoulders, nipped-in waist and typical 3 buttons of the 40s. Every decade reinvented the classic suit in its own way, but you can see 40s design elements cropping up in the 70s particularly, with wide lapels and accentuated waists, and in the 80s with the wide, padded shoulders and pleated skirts.

The photo below shows Doreen looking very smart in a similar outfit. These sturdy brown court shoes bear the CC41 utility label and would have been staple, everyday footwear made to last throughout the war. Note the high cut on the bridge of the foot, and the shape and height of the heel, making these quintessentially 40s.

The dress on this page is actually another from the 1980s. The 80s are a great resource for styling this 40s look. We've added a hand knit cardie and handbag to finish the look in the style of Madge, the lady in the picture. You could also carry a clutch bag like this early leather envelope bag, which would also work great here and look just like Madge.

Trousers were beginning to be more popular for work and leisure wear. for women during the 40s. These green wool, wide leg, high waisted slacks, also bear the CC41 utility label inside. Early trousers would have a side fastening, as shown here: a few buttons on the waistband and metal hook and eye fastenings. Zips were around but still not widely seen. This original Fair Isle tank top has some pre-ration button detailing. This many buttons wouldn't met CC41 standards! A Fair Isle tank top was also popular with men, and is an easy item to find to recreate a 40s look. In the photo you can see Midge in her high waisted slacks and blouse. She is also wearing white sandals, similar to those shown here. These are fantastic reproductions from Rocket Originals (website details at the back of the book)

Icons

1940s Icon – Carmen Miranda

When thinking of a 40s iconic look to recreate, we were rather spoilt for choice. There are so many Hollywood beauties with fabulous outfits to try and emulate, but no other actresses were quite as unique, eye-catching and instantly recognisable as Carmen Miranda. Who else wears fruit in their hair?! Her trademark fruit-hats were worn in the 1943 film *The Gang's All Here.*

This is one of Clare's favourite recreations and she turned heads in it at a vintage fair we organised. For this look you need to think big, bigger, and over the top with layering. For the base layer we've used a long, blue, 80s sequin skirt and a white Spanish-style off the shoulder top. Next we've added a piece of material, tucked in the skirt that looks like it's original fabric from a Mexican skirt, okay so it's not the right country (Miranda was a Portuguese-born, Brazilian) but the over all effect is very carnival-esque I'm sure you'll agree! Use this material to tuck into a belt (we've used a gold, pear-shaped belt to get more fruit in) to create volume, and you can also use it to create a bit of a train if it's long enough.

We've added a cropped, sequined waistcoat with gold trim and then lots and lots of jewellery, the more the merrier! Fill your arms up with bangles: wooden, painted, carved, bakelite if you have it or 'fakelite' plastic and metals, and hang as many different coloured and types of beads as your neck will hold!

The literal crowning glory is the fruit-turban. We've used a solid turban that had grapes and feathers already attached. It's fairly easy to pick up plastic fruit and to construct your own towering turban of fruit salad! Apparently Carmen made her own turban-hats so it's a good excuse to get creative.

Finally Clare is wearing some modern clear plastic mules with fruit in the heels and on the tops. 40s style high heels or platforms, like these reproduction red, Rocket Originals would do the trick. Make up wise, define and darken your brows, wear false eyelashes, lots of eye liner and big red, forties-shaped (go over your lips slightly at the edges to create the classic curved, wide mouth), big, red lips, courtesy of Rockalily Lipstick and voila! We-e-e-e like it ve-ery much!

Thicker brows with a defined arch, tapered to the outer end.

Eyeshadow wouldn't have been easy to get hold of so black eyeliner along the lash line and a neutral shade over the lid will be perfect, no cats eyes yet.

Matt red lipstick slightly over the upper lip line, widening the mouth from the corners and exaggerating the 'v' shape in the middle.

Look Book / Daywear

We've divided the 40s Look Books into seasons, so on this page we have a selection of more spring and summer pieces, whilst on the next page we have more autumn/winter items and colours.

Cream blouse with lace detail and painted pearl buttons.

Yellow, hand knitted original 40s cardigan. Knitwear was important for a 40s ladies' wardrobes. This has lovely details on the shoulders and pockets.

Sculpted back felt hat.

Red, white a blue, patriotic beads.

Handmade blouse. With handmade clothing you were free to embellish as you wished with whatever you had to hand, including extra covered buttons and embroidery like this one.

Original 40s felt floral brooch.

Pink cotton gingham suit.

Grey cardigan with patterned yoke.

White leather and woven, peep toe shoes, a pretty summer shoe.

Cream carved bangle.

56

Reproduction 'make do and mend' style felt brooches.

Pink hand knit cardigan.

Bakelite elephant brooch.

Yellow and purple floral dress with original belt and button detail.

Light grey suit, this was actually someone's war time wedding suit.

This is a hand embellished skirt with felt flowers, A lovely example of using the make do and mend ethic to jolly up a plain skirt.

Stylerite

Ear - Bobs

Red 'ear bobs' clip-on earrings on original cardboard backing

40s girdle, underwear became more structured in the 40s.

White sling-back, peep toe shoes. Note how 70s these look.

Genuine 40s seamed, nylon stockings. A highly coveted item in war torn Britain.

White, homemade felt gloves.

Brown leather peep toe shoes with bow detail.

Look Book / Daywear

Metal and plastic swan brooch.

Red leather gauntlet gloves. Gauntlets shapes were still popular during the 40s.

Felt 'tilt hat'.

Mustard open hang coat with button detail.

1980s peplum dress. The peplum dress is a classic 40s style. This 80s replica is perfect for achieving this look.

This maroon spotty dress is modern. This design is easy to get hold of and a popular one for 40s lovers as it has all the attributes we've talked about for a classic 40s dress.

Authentic military style, wool suit.

Navy leather clutch bag.

Navy scarf with floral edelweiss design.

Genuine 40s black, fleece lined boots, with a short practical heel.

V-neck hand knitted top. Multicoloured stripes were a popular look in the 40s as they were designed to use up odd scraps of wool.

Felt 'tilt hat'.

Original Pendleton '49er' jacket. Made in 1949 and popular during the 50s, this woollen jacket made by Pendleton in Oregon has been reproduced to the present day. The label shown here without a modern wool symbol, ensures this is an original 49er.

Green hand knit cardigan.

A selection of plastic and wooden bangles. Wear several bangles together for an American 40s look.

Mustard, handmade felt gloves.

These are reproduction 'saddle shoes' very popular in America during the 40s and 50s. These are made by Rocket Originals.

Red and white reproduction knitted top, based on an original 40s design by Rocket originals.

A pair of original 40s sunglasses.

These are great US style reproduction jeans made by Freddies of Pinewood. Wear with a Pendleton and saddle shoes for the ultimate casual US 40s look!

A pair of reproduction 'Remix' lace up, peep toe wedges.

Black alligator style boxy handbag.

Bamboo bangle.

Look Book / Eveningwear

If you needed a glamourous evening dress in the early 40s, especially in Britain, you were very lucky indeed! These evening items show the stylish to the downright extravagant.

Plastic and carved bangles.

This fun 40s gold coloured compact is mostly likely American and features a romantic design of uniformed courting couples.

Marcasite and pearl brooch.

Demure black evening dress with embroidered flower design.

Peach evening gloves with gold embroidery detail.

Small evening bag, homemade, cardboard clutch with loop fastening.

Colourful, highly patterned dress with matching capelet.

Blue and gold suede dancing shoes.

Handbag with a smart diamante detailed clasp.

Gold CC41 dancing shoes.

Snake skin bag.

Red satin evening gloves.

Cotton summer, off-the-shoulder gown with bright green print.

Man made fibre, print dress in bold yellow, pinks and purples. Quite a head turner.

Black and gold drawstring handbag.

Smart black veiled hat with handmade felt flower detail. Perfect for a formal evening function.

Blue velvet evening dress with a clear example of what is known as the 'sweetheart' neckline. The two curves on the chest look like the top of a heart.

1950s

The glamourous and exaggeratedly feminine fashions of the 1950s seemed the perfect antidote to the austere and sensible fashions of the war years.

The 50s were dominated by two main shapes for women: the full skirt introduced by Dior in 1947, a quintessential style of the decade, and the straight or wiggle-skirted look. You could define these two looks as either the Doris Day or the Marilyn Monroe look. Both required a cinched in, accentuated waist so the hour glass figure became the aspirational shape for women of the 50s, requiring new and more rigid undergarments to achieve it. This saw a revival of the corset, hip padding and the invention of the pointy, mind-it-doesn't-take-your-eye-out, bullet bra. Some women rejected what they saw as a big step backwards for women's liberation, going from the factories back into the kitchen as a corseted wife and mother.

The 50s witnessed the birth of the 'teenager': it was an exciting time to be young. Before this time teens just wore smaller versions of their parents clothing, a notion universally rejected by this Rock 'n' Roll infused generation. Boys and girls would have left school at fourteen and had money to spend, so it didn't take long for more mainstream fashion to become youth conscious and cash in on this new, affluent market. Teens were all dolled up in fashion ranges just for them, out on the town, jiving at the Milk Bar.

The new youth culture with its rebellious attitude, brought about a further relaxing of previously formal dress codes: these new teens didn't want to dress or act like their parents so items like hats which were associated with their elders and conformity were spurned by the younger generation, particularly men. Jeans, formerly workwear, and t-shirts, previously only underwear, were popularized thanks to Hollywood and the influence of film stars such as James Dean and Marlon Brando. Younger women would now also be wearing jeans, pedal pushers or capri pants, or narrow cigarette pants, all with a high waist.

More mature women still wouldn't have worn trousers for anything other than sports or gardening. It was quite a prim and proper decade for ladies, and required excellent grooming. Women's clothing was still highly accessorised during the 50s, and respectable ladies wouldn't be seen out without their hats, often pillbox shaped, gloves, and matching handbags and shoes. Stilettos were the new heels to be seen tottering about in.

Cats-eye shaped glasses were a new invention of the 50s and almost universally adopted, in prescription eyewear and sunglasses.

Fashion subcultures and 'tribes' arrived for the first time. Teddy Boys, Teddy Girls and beatniks, would pave the way for the mods, rockers and punks of later years.

There was an explosion of new culture, especially music and art, and televisions began appearing in homes, opening people's eyes to the bigger picture.

Beatniks were a more arty and intellectual youth movement originating in New York. Clothing associated with beatniks includes black tapered trousers, worn with black turtlenecks, stripy tops or crop tops, and with flip flops or flat pumps.

The arrival of, and growing interest in, nuclear power was reflected in fabric designs for clothing and soft furnishing which became more colourful and daring. 'Atomic prints' is the name given to designs inspired by the new futuristic, atomic age.

For most people today, when you talk of vintage dresses the classic 50s cotton frock is what springs to mind. These crisp, cotton, full-skirted numbers with big, poofy petticoats, is a look that lasted well into the early 60s.

These original dresses are now highly prized in the vintage world and have seen a revival in their cuts and shapes in recent years due to the influence of TV shows set in the 50s/60s. We've included a double page of some of our favourite 50s cotton dresses here.

This is one of the easiest looks to recreate using non-authentic dresses, thanks to the 50s style revival of the 80s. Look for cotton or lightweight polyester dresses with buttons to the waist and a fuller skirt, or circle or dirndl skirts worn with a blouse. In the shop people are often fretting that they can't fit into original 50s frocks due to the narrow, fitted waist. This is where we have to be reminded that women would have been wearing constrictive foundation wear to achieve the hourglass shape. To recreate this look authentically it is worth investing in a decent petticoat and original or reproduction underwear (corset and bullet bra) to create the perfect 50s silhouette.

50

" *Frock around the clock* "

Workwear

This is an outfit for a working 50s woman. It consists of a black, reproduction wiggle/pencil skirt and an original heavy cotton gingham blouse. The 50s was the era of the pointy bullet bra, here's one of the cone-shaped wonders. A wide belt to accentuate your hourglass figure is imperative for the 50s silhouette. Smart ladies about town wouldn't be seen without their hat and gloves, here's black lace pair and with a woven bow detail hat. Boxy handbags were a 50s staple and this sexy secretary look is finished off with original kitten heels and cat's eye glasses, meow!

1950s

Teen Fashion

Here are some examples of teen fashions. We've included a man's 'Teddy Boy' drape coat and 'brothel creepers' shoes as they are such iconic looks.

We've also put together a lesser-known 'Teddy Girl' look, which we think is a really great alternative 50s outfit. It takes elements from the male version but adds feminine touches such as a cameo brooch worn at the neck, often with a bow behind it. They often wore long, riding style jackets with velvet collars, similar to the 80s jacket shown here. Teddy girls wore either pencil skirts or jeans with turn-ups. Here are a pair of original 50s blue jeans. They still fasten at the side but with a zip and are more tapered than 40s jeans. They look great rolled up to capri length!

On the mannequin are a pair of modern, 50s style tapered 'cigarette pants' which were a popular new style of trousers for young women. Modern day ballet pump shoes finish off a youthful 50s look a treat.

Eveningwear

This is a more formal, elegant 50s evening wear with all original elements. A fur stole, whether real or faux, (faux fur grew in popularity in the 50s) is an authentic, luxurious alternative to an evening coat.

50s evening hats were small and often 'half moon' shaped. This feathered one unfurls and cups the back of the head, with netting falling over the face.

We've accessorised the taffeta, striped evening dress with original gold shoes, which show the move to a thinner, higher stiletto heel. There are long purple evening gloves to match the dress and coordinating iridescent earrings. The gold brooch could be worn on the stole and matches the shoes and metal handle of the evening bag.

1950s

This is a slightly more Rock 'n' Roll evening outfit with one of our favourite dresses, which has an unusual scalloped neckline and oriental fishing print.

We've teamed it with matching red and blue accessories. Gloves and hats are still a big part of the 50s ladies' wardrobe. This felt evening hat has subtle curves that give it an almost 'clam' shape and would be worn at the back of the head. The blue leather stilettos match the blue bag, bangle and 'aurora borealis' rhinestone clip-on earrings.

Cotton Dresses

Pretty cotton dresses with large, petticoat enhanced skirts are for some people the definitive look of the 50s, they were also popular well into the 60s. Here we have a selection of genuine dresses that range from early to late 50s. Note the subtle differences in the style and shapes of the collars, for instance, wider lapels and shirtwaist dresses were usually from earlier in the decade, with strapless or sleeveless, boat neck designs coming later. They were available in all colours and patterns including stripes, spots, florals and ginghams as seen here.

Get the Look

In the first photo we have a great example of the classic 50s look: a belted, patterned skirt with a tucked in top. On this page we have recreated this popular look by using an 80s cotton skirt. As well as 40s inspired styles, the 80s had a big 50s revival and 80s clothes can provide some handy alternatives to pricy original items, with authentic looking skirts and dresses. We can't stress enough how important the petticoat is for a 50s silhouette, they are a good investment piece if you really want to look the part.

With our grey checked skirt, we've picked out the red in the print to get a match with an original 50s belt, a chiffon neck scarf and red gloves. The white cotton top is actually a 60s sports top, and for an easy shoes option go with ankle socks and some modern lace up canvas pumps which are really easy to get hold of. Small hoop earrings were popular in the 50s and work nicely to finish this look. Cottons were key fabrics for everyday wear in the 50s, synthetics hadn't hit the high street yet, so stick to natural fibres for an authentic appearance.

On this page we can see more fabulous 50s patterned skirts in the photos. We love Betty's can-can girls print, Dawn's stripes and squares and Verna's delicate flower print.

Poodles are a recurring emblem in 50s fashion. This is an original pink poodle skirt which just needs a poofy petticoat underneath for the perfect rock 'n' roll look. As you can also see from the photos, wicker bags were a popular accessory in the 50s. We've used a round, record shaped one, which adds to the youthful feel to this ensemble.

Get the Look

As we've said, cotton dresses epitomise 50s style for most people. Flowers and spots are key prints and here we have a photo of Auntie Di in a spotty cotton number. She's accessorised with little lace gloves and completes the summery look with a straw shopper. We've picked out two dresses in similar styles. Horrockses were a big name in the UK for printed cotton dresses, and their label is worth looking out for. HIghly collectible today, because of their brightly coloured prints on high quality fabric.

To get this look choose a dress with a cinched in waist and full skirt, wear with a petticoat to create a voluminous 50s silhouette.

This smart grey coat and hat are reminiscent of cousin Valerie's 'New Look' style 50s wedding suit, as seen in the photo. To achieve this look choose a coat with a fitted waist and flared skirt. Colours to look for are pastels, dove grey and creams, where possible match your hat with the coat and gloves for a polished look.

50s evening gowns followed the style of the day dresses, but were longer and in more luxurious fabrics. This is a heavy, turquoise satin brocade gown perfect for whirling around the dance floor. They would be worn with a long stiff petticoat or have one built in to shape the skirt, and the bodice would be boned or worn with a corset. There was a lot of 'help' going on underneath a 50s dress to achieve a smooth graceful line, so period style underwear should be considered when going for this look.

In the photo Betty has accessorised her black evening gown with dainty, pale pink, long evening gloves which finish this formal evening look . Her dress is embellished with beading but often dress clips or diamante brooches would be attached to add the sparkle. These cat's eye glasses, just like Betty's are vintage frames from Dead Men's Spex. Vintage eyewear is a great way to add the finishing touch to a look, Betty would love them! You can have your own lenses added to glasses like these to have a 50s face every day.

1950s

Icons

1950s Icon – Marilyn Monroe

For us Marilyn Monroe epitomizes 50s glamour. Her mix of sex appeal and vulnerability gained her gazillions of fans worldwide and is probably still as popular and as famous today as she ever was.

Her most notorious dress is the white pleated, halter neck as worn in the Seven Year Itch. You can pick these up from fancy dress shops and costume hire places fairly easily. We wanted to recreate her look using less obvious but still iconic elements. She was often photographed in strappy or strapless wiggle dresses and that's the look we've gone for here.

This was a fun one to do, who wouldn't like to dress up as Marilyn Monroe?! Clare's modelling an 80s green, strapless, sequined cocktail dress with a large sash. Worn with long, white evening gloves and lots of sparkly jewellery: if Marilyn taught us anything it's that diamonds are a girl's best friend! Clare's wearing a diamante necklace and matching diamante bracelet cuffs.

We've also used a 50s style, leopard print evening coat worn over the shoulders and some 80s gold mules – Marilyn's shoe of choice.

The hair and make up is a big part of the look as always, and we've used a modern, 70s style wig, which when pinned up at the back emulates Marilyn's 50s 'set' look. Use a light coloured eyeshadow and highlighters under the brow, pencil your eyebrows thicker, add cats-eye eyeliner, and red lips. Last but by no means least, don't forget to put on your beauty spot!

1950s

Thicker eyebrows are fashionable, well shaped with a strong arch, use a sharp eye pencil to keep it well defined.

It has to be the classic 'cats eye' shaped eye liner, steady hand needed to draw a smooth line along the upper lashes thickening towards the outer eye with a 'flick' at the end.

Think big on the lips, Marilyn famously wore red, but pinks were also popular, use liner to go a little outside your lip line, not too far out, but just enough to give an extra luscious pout!

A healthy glow was beginning to be popular so a light brush with bronzer or a skin tone face powder to set your look will finish things off perfectly.

Look Book / Daywear

There were lots of different styles and silhouettes to chose from in the 50s. Here we have a cross-section of daywear illustrating the different looks you could achieve.

Pillbox hats were the defining hat style of the decade, whether straw, fur print or felt. Leopard print, pillbox faux fur hat

Green striped wool blouse.

Black leather waist belt.

Cream, three button 50s woollen coat.

Marcasite boat brooch

Original 50s blue and black check wool dress.

Oblong cane handbag.

Gingham cropped, tie blouse.

Sensible brown work shoes.

Yellow and brown wool check bag and matching headscarf.

Elasticated red belt.

Carpet style floral handbag.

Pink felt hat with feathers.

Black leather box-shaped handbags.

Marcasite rose brooch.

Cropped tartan, wool jacket.

Early 50s grey-brown leather shoes.

Green straw beret.

Cotton blossom print dress.

Pink two-piece, belted dress and duster jacket.

Plastic pearl clip-on earrings.

White petticoat with layers of tulle.

Brown and white leather day shoe.

Red and black checked, wool pencil skirt from the 80s. A great example of achieving the 50s look with non-authentic items.

Raffia handbag with bamboo cane handle.

Look Book / Leisurewear

The youth market was a big growth area during the 50s and young people wanted to have fun, especially with fashion. Here we have a selection of leisure clothes, inspiration for how to achieve a fun, youthful 50s holiday look.

Red straw coolie hat.

Plastic fruit clip-on earrings.

Original 50s flip flops.

Baby blue 'lobster bag' basket, reminiscent of a fishing basket made from cane and net.

Cotton, red and white print tunic top.

Checked, cotton wrap dress.

Glass fruit necklace.

Shell-shaped wicker bag with plastic wrapped handle.

Original green cat's eye sunglasses.

Floral patterned, turquoise cotton skirt worn with coordinating cotton blouse.

Bull fighting themed bracelet. Souvenir, novelty jewellery was a holiday favourite and a fun accessory.

Modern red straw wedges, but a great replica for a popular beach shoe of the time.

Yellow plastic, button earrings.

Towelling beach top with boating design.

Straw coolie with embroidered detail.

Knitted nautical striped top with anchor pocket. Popular since the 20s, striped Breton tops were often worn with pedal pushers. This one is actually from the 80s.

Diamante detail original cat's eye sunglasses.

Cotton cropped bolero with cap sleeves.

Polka dots were popular, this scarf could be worn on the head, around the neck or in a top pocket.

Original baby blue swimming costume, note the low modest leg, the halter neck strap is detachable.

Unusual cotton towelling beach cover-up decorated with bank notes from around the world.

Another great 50s printed cotton skirt, this time an Oriental fan design.

Swan hair clip.

Cane box handbag.

Leather wedges.

Wicker bag decorated with bright, embroidered wool leaves.

Look Book / Eveningwear

Clothing in the 50s seemed to offer a touch of Hollywood glamour for all. Whether a cocktail wiggle dress Marilyn style, or a full length ball gown like Princess Grace, the ladies of the 50s knew how to look their best for a night out.

Diamante starburst brooch.

Net covered, 'half moon' hat worn on the back of the head.

Faux fur evening coat with big funnel collar.

Orangey-red taffeta silk dress.

Plum satin party dress.

Faux fur leopard pencil skirt.

Red satin evening gown with rose pattern.

Gold leather strappy evening shoes.

Velvet bow hat with net to cover face.

Patent blue pointy stilettos.

Diamante grape clip-on earrings.

Lace embroidered black wiggle dress.

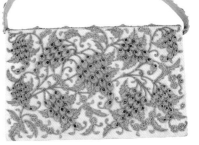
Embroidered gold and beaded handbag.

Pearl purse.

Green wiggle dress with beaded bodice.

Marcasite flower brooch.

Lace overlay three-quarter length sleeve dress.

Black velvet hat with feather adornment.

Faux leopard coat.

Two pearl hat pins.

Long, embroidered pastel green gloves.

Lace and velvet ball gown.

Navy leather stilettos.

Tulle cocktail dress with lace appliquéd flowers, worn with fur cape.

"You're not going out like that!" was most likely echoed throughout the land as fathers despaired of their daughters in the new mini skirt.

The 1960s really saw the youth culture kick started in the 50s reach its zenith. It was another revolutionary decade as the post-war baby boomers came of age, fought for equal rights and wanted a fashion movement to call their own.

It was the first time that young people designed and sold clothes for themselves and their age group. Accessories in the 60s reflected the new and fun approach to fashion with lots of brightly coloured plastics. Due to mass production of ready-to-wear garments, 60s shoppers were spoilt for choice.

The emphasis was on youthfulness, looking womanly was passé: the hourglass figure was out. Fashion embraced the more youthful 'Twiggy' shape more akin to that of the 20s: tall and flat chested. The 20s influence could also be seen in some of the drop waist designs of the era, the sharp bobs and 'Eton crops' and the 'Mary Jane' shoes of the time.

Clothing shapes and silhouettes were simplified in the 60s, and the A-line shift dress was the shape that defined that period, suiting the taller, leggier 60s model figure: bad luck curvy girls!

The mini skirt was the phenomenon of the 60s, seeing hemlines rising to shocking new heights. Aided and abetted by the invention of tights/pantyhose that came in new and exciting colours. As skirts got shorter, heels became lower and squarer, and apparently everyone was talking about those kinky boots!

We're overheating at the very thought of all the synthetic fabrics on offer in the 60s. Polyester, nylon, vinyl and PVC were popular and Crimplene was the fabric of the decade: a thick polyester that was easy to wear, care for and also easy to sew with. Making your own clothing was as popular as ever, and ladies could whip up a quick Crimplene shift dress, in all manner of colours and patterns. We've some homemade examples in the following pages. You can easily pick up Crimplene dresses today and they are often the cheaper items on a vintage rail: this stuff lasts forever!

Following on from the atomic age was the space age of the 60s, and fashion took inspiration from the space race that culminated in the moon landings of 1969. Silver and gold metallics were incorporated into statement dresses. The futuristic designs coming out of the high-end fashion houses featuring metals and chainmail, were eventually reflected in the ready to wear, off the peg designs of high street stores.

Geometric shapes in colours or black and whites inspired fabric and fashion designers, especially Mary Quant, whose two-tone, black and white mini dresses are icons of the era.

Youth fashion tribes formed sides as mods and rockers. Mods were image conscious and sharply dressed in their tailored suits, dresses and two-pieces; rockers were a scruffier bunch, rebels in their jeans, t-shirts and the obligatory leather jacket. There was also the bohemian art school set, related to the beatniks of the previous decade but more avant-garde and experimental. Many of the young trail blazers in art and music were from art schools or collectives in the UK and US, most famously Andy Warhol's Factory set.

Music was a huge influence on fashion and as the 60s progressed, psychedelic patterns and prints were introduced. In the latter part of the decade the 'hippie' movement that began the US, infiltrated youth fashion and trends throughout the West. 'Flower power' and the hippie look would also go on to inform a lot of the style elements of the next decade.

"One small step for mankind, one giant leap for fashion."

Early 60s Daywear

These are two outfits from the early 60s. You can see the 50s influence, designs from before the 60s had fully 'swung'. This smart day look is our homage to style icon Jackie O, back when she was First Lady Jackie Kennedy. It's a baby blue suit with a square fur collar. The fake fabric button details on the jacket are a nice touch. The key to this look is to look fresh, matching and polished. We've teamed it with a quirky matching felt hat, her trademark big sunglasses and matching white shoes, bag and gloves.

We love the colours in this knee-length wiggle dress, with side drape detail. This is the perfect 'day to evening' outfit. The geometric patterned flat shoes, and smart alligator-style bag give it more of a day look, but the cropped satin jacket would transform it to an evening look, especially with the almost perfectly matched earrings. Afterwork cocktails anyone?

Daywear

What a difference a few years can make, this bright, youthful outfit uses colour blocking and quirky jewellery to give it an unmistakable swinging 60s look, a far cry from the prim and proper outfits before. This is a crocheted shift dress, most likely homemade, and is a vibrant colour-fest when joined by this original short yellow mac and matching yellow straw, cloche-style hat. The 60s exaggerated style elements such as colours, jewellery, and eyelashes for looks that created impact. The plastic jewellery here includes large beaded earrings, and 'Pop-it' bead necklaces which could be shortened or lengthened and different colours added by literally popping them in and out. We've also included a fun, furry metal chick brooch, a great example of the novelty pieces from the time. These two-tone slingbacks are typical of the era, shoes had flat heels and square toes in the 60s.

Although the 60s were synonymous with bright colours, black and white were also big news. This is an iconic black and white mini dress outfit, a style made famous by Mary Quant. For most people we meet who are looking for a classic 60s look, this is what they have in mind. This is a 90s-does-60s reproduction dress but the rest of the items are original. As hemlines got shorter, thanks to the invention of tights (a genuine Mary Quant tights box can be seen here) boots got longer. These PVC kinky boots would go over the knee. We've matched the shiny boots with a shiny patent box bag. We've kept the jewellery minimal with black button earrings. A 20s flapper-style, sharp bob haircut is a must with this look!

1960s

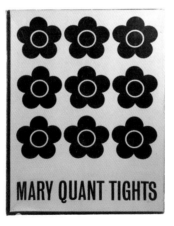

MARY QUANT TIGHTS

Eveningwear

This more sophisticated evening outfit shows textures popular in this era such as lace, beading and unusual plastic earrings. The textures add interest to this all black look but you could always jazz up this outfit with the addition of a pair of coloured tights. This original lace dress is a 'baby doll' style, fitted under the bust for an empire line. We've added a raffia, beaded evening bag to add another texture, and these typically 60s-shaped shoes are satin with rhinestone flower detail. With the high neck of the dress and these fun, over-sized beaded earrings with a hint of sparkle, no other jewellery would be necessary. Eyes were emphasised and exaggerated in the 60s with bold eyeliner and large fake eyelashes give a helping hand.

The advancement in synthetics and fabric production brought about new metallic clothing, perfectly timed for the 60s space obsession, culminating in the moon landings in '69. This is a metallic silver, woven, all-in-one with wide-legged culottes, which are just visible. We've gone for a head to toe silver look with a matching lame bag with a space age metal handle, and lamé shoes. Both the shoes and the large butterfly brooch contain 'Aurora Borealis' crystals, so called because of their multi-coloured sparkles. This outfit would be a real head turner!

Get the Look

The mini skirt is one of the most iconic pieces of the 60s era. The photographs on these pages show different ways the mini skirt was worn and some of the different lengths, from over the knee to the top of the thigh! This suede mini skirt and top is a typical look. We can see similar looks on Pam and Lynne from 1969, although they are wearing a jersey two-piece and knitted dress respectively. We've teamed our suede mini with a green check polyester top and co-ordinating brown patent bag.

In an earlier photo below from '67, there's a clear example on the mini dress, of the fantastic prints that were abound in the 60s. We've found a towelling lined, zip-up mini dress with a slightly more psychedelic print, as this one was intended for holiday wear.

On the opposite page we have some great examples in the photos of mini skirt suits from the later 60s. These photos are from a family wedding and you can see the latest fashions were even worn to formal occasions. Our blue mini suit is reminiscent of the suits below, it's double breasted with a wool trim collar, so more suited to a cooler occasion. The blue hat here with the bow, is almost identical to Helen's in the photo. These were a popular late 60s design that was also around in the following decade.

On the top of the page we have an example of an early 60s printed cotton dress. It's taking some of its design elements from the 50s, but the sleeveless shift style is typically 60s. This dress had actually been shortened to give it an above the knee, 60s look. The pattern and style of dress in the photo resembles the one shown here.

Get the Look

More mini skirts and dresses here, but this time we're in The Avengers territory with this fantastic, futuristic leather wrap mini dress with metal fasteners. It's another example of the different fabric textures of the 60s. Wear leather with a knitted top, like Pam in the photo, along with some long 'love beads'.

Leggings, ski pants or stirrup pants, the tight fitting stretchy jersey trousers with a loop or stirrup at the bottom, are more recently associated with 80s fashion, but were in fact popularised in the 60s as more youthful leisure wear. On the opposite page, we have a great example of this casual look, with Caz in her ski pants, Aran knit cardie and 'Dr Scholl' wooden sandals. All these items are everyday design classics in their own right. Aran knits are as popular today as they ever were and Dr Scholl sandals are still being made in the exact same style. Photos like this are so interesting as an illustration of the cyclical nature of fashion and timeless classic designs of everyday clothing that have spanned the decades.

On the lower right, we can see Midge in her 60s summer shift dress, another example of colourful prints and patterns. We've recreated a similar beach outfit with this floral patterned tunic dress and oversized 60s style sunglasses. We've also added a later belt worn on the hips to break up the pattern and accessorise the outfit.

ICONS

1960s Icon – Edie Sedgwick

Edie Sedgwick optimised 60s cool. She was an actress, model and all round 'It Girl', most famous for her collaborations with Andy Warhol. She was part of a pioneering group of artists and actors who defined the swinging 60s in the US.

We've recreated one of her classic looks here: opaque black tights with a striped top and large, oversized gold earrings. Her trademark was her huge earrings. We found a modern pair just like the sort she used to wear. She also clipped gold earrings together to make a chain of bigger, longer earrings which we've replicated. We've also used black leggings instead of tights and a modern, striped t-shirt to show how you can recreate this look easily, but have used a genuine 1960s metallic, gold waistcoat to give the overall look authenticity.

Wear heavy eye makeup including thick brows, smudgy, cats-eye eyeliner with thick false lashes. Use white or a light eye shadow or highlighter. No need for lipstick for this look. Although Jo hasn't got Edie's blonde hair, she has styled her hair for the era with a bit of back combing.

Shoe-wise a simple, flat pump would work or go shoeless as she was often photographed barefoot.

We've finished this look with a 1960s black, beaded and sequined evening bag.

We like Edie Sedgwick as she was innovative with her unusual, artsy, bohemian, style. This is an easy outfit to recreate but also very distinctive.

Edie had very thick penciled in eyebrows, this was her look so don't be scared to really sculpt yourself some statement brows with an eyebrow pencil over your natural shape.

Thick bold colours were typical for eyes: whites, creams, black and blue eyeshadows with a graphic highlight of the eye socket and all around the eye line. Use a black eyeshadow and eye pencil to literally draw a line around the eye socket and blend. Go heavy on the eyeliner with exaggerated cats eyes.

False eyelashes are a must, even layer two pairs!

Lips were not the focal point, emphasis was on the eyes so you can even use concealer on your lips or wear a pale pink colour.

Look Book / Dresses

Vibrant patterned dresses are a significant look of the era, we've grouped some fantastic, different examples together. Crimplene was the revolutionary synthetic fabric of the decade that saw a new hey day with the mass production of clothing. Dresses made from Crimplene came in all colours and patterns.

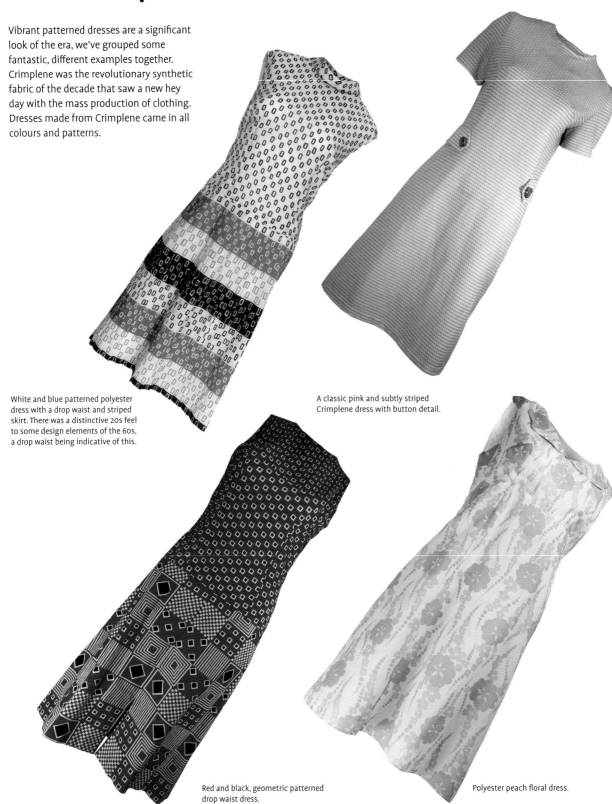

White and blue patterned polyester dress with a drop waist and striped skirt. There was a distinctive 20s feel to some design elements of the 60s, a drop waist being indicative of this.

A classic pink and subtly striped Crimplene dress with button detail.

Red and black, geometric patterned drop waist dress.

Polyester peach floral dress.

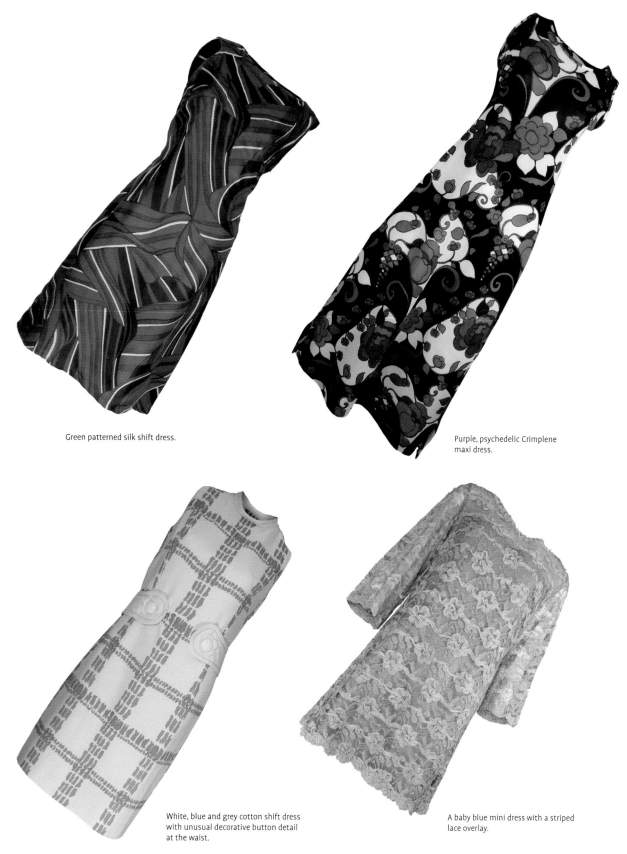

Green patterned silk shift dress.

Purple, psychedelic Crimplene maxi dress.

White, blue and grey cotton shift dress with unusual decorative button detail at the waist.

A baby blue mini dress with a striped lace overlay.

Look Book / Daywear

We've split our day wear into two sections, concentrating on reds and dark colours here, with more of a mix of pastels and earth tones on the next page. Capes were a particular trend on the 60s and we've included a couple of our favourites here.

Red, hand knit wool beret. Apparently the film Bonnie & Clyde in 1967 resulted in a spike in beret sales.

Classic checked hat.

A fun, jewelled bird brooch.

Macs are an all time classic item, with subtle design tweaks for each new decade. This is an original 60s version.

Black leather handbag.

Woollen checked coat with furry crossover collar.

Mohair tartan shawl/capelet.

Blue and red two-piece: matching shift dress and jacket.

Red plastic button earrings.

Multi-coloured beaded clutch bag.

Leopard print cape.

Black mohair hat.

20s inspired, grey 'Mary Jane' shoes. The low, square heel is the 60s giveaway.

Reversible woollen tartan cape.

Red and black vinyl shopper with zip features.

Black, button up jersey mini dress.

Blackwatch tartan and patent holdall.

Look Book / Daywear

Vinyl and tapestry bag.

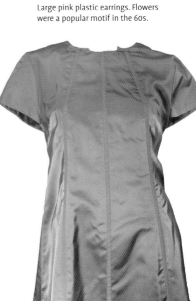

Large pink plastic earrings. Flowers were a popular motif in the 60s.

Quirky felt hat.

Satin mini dress.

White spotted mini skirt with matching belt.

Chanel-style suits were a big trend in the 60s, you can just imagine the Audrey Hepburn wannabes, fully accessorised, in this suit.

Bronze lamé shoes.

Small black handbag.

Pink plastic beads.

Crimplene turtleneck mod top.

Pink geometric patterned mini shirtdress.

This ladies' tweed mod suit is a slightly later version and also came with a matching skirt. With a gingham blouse underneath this is the perfect, sharp-suited mod attire.

An interesting pink, gingham, nylon mod shirt with unusual button-down collar.

A purple patent bag .

Felt bowler hat with purple felt trim.

Look Book / Eveningwear

We've dedicated this evening section to blue hues and space age sparkles. Baby blue was a popular shade in the 60s.

Lamé evening bag with short chain handle.

Silver crocheted clutch bag.

Sophisticated dark blue silk ball gown, with a drop waist and full maxi skirt.

White and turquoise embellished maxi gown.

Blue blow and ruffle detail, chiffon overlay mini dress.

Light blue mini dress with drop waist and silvery waistband detailing.

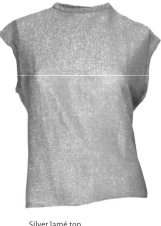

Silver lamé top.

Baby blue button earrings.

An exquisitely beaded, wide-necked top.

High neck, empire line mini dress with beading detail.

Large faux pearl and bead statement necklace.

Silver handbag with chain handle.

20s inspired layered, ruffle baby doll micro-mini dress

Gold lamé and glittery bag.

Baby blue polyester dress with lacy top and front bow detail.

White and silver lamé knit mini shift dress

1970s

There was a lot going on in 1970s fashion, people had the freedom to express themselves leading to diverse trends from the hippie, trippy, handmade look to the spandex, disco sisters.

After the mini skirt phenomenon of the 60s, the 70s brought with it a new invention called hot pants, but on the whole hemlines drastically dropped with new midi and maxi lengths. Dresses were significantly longer and flowing, with straight or empire lines often with tiers and layers with bell or balloon sleeves. There was still a lot of static in the air as lighter-weight polyester and chiffon were the go-to fabrics for affordable fashion. Maxi dresses are possibly one of the most collectible and wearable fashions of the 70s, we've included some of our favourites from the shop in the following pages.

The hippie movement of the late 60s influenced much of the 70s with a shift to a more ethnic look. There were Indian cottons and African inspired prints and designs such as the kaftan. The package holiday boom also gave us some of these international influences and more, including the iconic 'safari suit' and dresses.

Girls got back to their roots with a big handicrafts resurgence, which went hand in hand with the individualism of the ethnic, hippie trend. There were a lot of hand-crocheted dresses, belts and bags, tie-dye and batik-ed clothing being worn.

The ultra modern, forward-looking designs of the 60s were replaced with a retrospective nostalgia in the 70s. There was a 30s revival and interestingly, some of the 70s key trends: the large collars and flared trousers were first invented in the 30s, but only those at the top of the high fashion tree would have worn them back then. The London fashion house and department store Biba wore their 30s influence literally on their sleeves, with their deco inspired prints and bias-cut dresses. There was also a Victorian influence visible with high neck collars on blouses on 'Prairie' and 'Granny' dresses.

The 70s saw a further relaxing of all previous clothing formalities for younger men and women. Jeans for all were here to stay and were either flared or tight and tucked into knee boots. Hard-wearing fabrics such as denim, suede and corduroy were popular and seen as skirts, dungarees, jacket and even suits.

Designers must've thought the bigger the better, with oversized collars, flared trousers and exaggerated, platform heels becoming almost universal. Hairstyles also reflected this whether they were super long locks, bouncing afros or frou-frou flicks (remember Farrah Fawcett from TV show *Charlie's Angels*?).

Music, film and celebrity continued to influence designers and the populace, with disco and glam rock inspired clothes sparkling and shimmering on the dance floor. There were also androgynous, unisex styles for men and women.

The longevity of trends from this era shows that there's more to the 70s than the cartoonish 'costume party' stereotypes. This could be because the 70s was the first era to borrow significantly from design elements of previous decades, creating new classics. In the shop we often recreate looks from as far back as the 20s with items from the 70s, which show the variety and versatility of clothing from this period.

The late 70s witnessed the ultimate youth rebellion in the UK, in the form of punk. The middle classes were horrified by the anti-establishment attitudes, and DIY fashion packed a punch featuring zips, rips, bones and pins. As a fashion sub-culture punks were rarely seen outside of big cities and didn't influence mainstream, everyday fashion at the time, although its impact on fashion in general was in fact long lasting.

The late 70s also saw the birth of the tracksuit as the ultimate in relaxed, comfortable daywear. This would soon become the next big thing.

"Turn on, tune in and drop your hemline"

Daywear

Earth tones such as browns and greens were popular colours in the 70s. Here we have a pair of heavy, tapestry flares, worn with a polyester pink pussy bow blouse and green suede waistcoat. Accessorised with a handmade carpet bag, furry felt hat and a humungous pair of platform sandals. This outfit would not be for shy and retiring types! This particular look also illustrates the androgynous trend of the decade: colourful, frilly shirts, waistcoats and flares would have been seen on both men and women.

Another colourful look, here we have a floral print maxi skirt, the bold, psychedelic hippie-style patterns of the late 60s carried over well into the 70s. This outfit consists of a bright yellow pussy bow blouse, but just as often you will see long, pointy collars on tops. We've teamed it with a velvet jacket and cloth-style cap, plus a big brown leather handbag and coordinating platform shoes.

Holiday wear

During the 70s package holidays abroad became much more affordable and as folk flew across the seas to enjoy the sun they acquired a whole new wardrobe of leisure and tourist wear.

On the mannequin is a classic cotton safari dress with a leather-look tie belt, leopard print scarf and straw safari hat.

The big trend for kaftans in the 70s came directly from the holiday boom. This kaftan is a pleated, floral delight, its lack of shape makes it one size fits all.

On this page we also have a floppy cotton sun hat, a plasticised, fringed beach bag and an early 70s leopard print bikini for the beach babe.

Here we have some examples of leather souvenir items. The souvenir trade was brisk during the 70s, but you didn't have to return home with a sombrero or a model donkey. These painted and tooled leather purses and Egyptian-themed satchel bag are actually pretty tasteful.

70s swimwear commonly had a flattering low cut leg, and came in an variety of plain or typical period floral print designs. Bikinis were worn to get that popular 70s tan too, daring hipster bottoms were the choice for the young and beautiful.

The psychedelic, polyester orange and yellow two-piece, beach coverup is a pretty special outfit. Heads will turn when you go for an ice-cream in that.

1970s

Maxi Dresses

Maxi dresses are one of the key looks of the 70s. All ages would've worn them and these kinds of dresses are still popular today. They came in all colours and prints, made from cotton, chiffon, velvet or polyester, often with layers, tiers, ruffles, in empire lines, with halter necks, or billowy long sleeves, just to describe a few! We've put together a small cross-section here.

Green floral, 30s style (it's the butterfly sleeves again) maxi with bottom tier.

Tiered top, floral dress.

Purply-blue empire line chiffon maxi with big bell sleeves.

This is another 30s throwback with a Deco inspired print. It's reminiscent of a 'Biba-style' dress.

Strappy multi-coloured check maxi.

Halter neck maxi with 'Pucci' style geometric print.

Eveningwear

Jumpsuits took off in the 70s. Here we have a 'Biba inspired' exotic outfit. Although all authentic 70s, the wide legs show a 30s influence, while the turban and shoes are distinctly 40s.

The sparkle and glitz of disco and glam rock influenced fashion for all ages. This more sophisticated 70s outfit has glitter in every element.

Get the Look

There are so many trends in the 70s to cover, it was a melting pot of design elements from previous decades. Highly patterned fabrics were everywhere in 70s home wares and on clothes for adults and children alike, as can be seen in the photo on this smart little chap's matching shirt and tie combo! We've found a 'looky-likey' dress with a pussy bow tie, which is typical of the patterns of the era.

Denim was a big feature in the 70s. The former work wear was now here to stay. Double denim, in tops and bottoms - on men and women was also a popular new trend for this decade. Here we have a pale double denim suit with classic 70s big collars and some embroidery detailing on the shirt and flares. Nice! You could add a chunky brown leather belt to this to further finish the look. You could add sew-on patches to your jeans or shirt for classic 70s embellishment, which was also popular at the time.

Hippie tops and denim flares were popular for women as can also be seen here in the photos. We've recreated the look with authentic 70s floral tie-neck top and flared jeans. As these photos show clearly, clothes were worn tight, showing off your figure was key for men and women.

Here's another example of a maxi dress, this time it's made from cotton with tiers akin to those in the photo. People always think of platforms for footwear, but strappy sandals were popular for women. This snakeskin pair would have been lovely with this dress and fab at the disco, plus much easier to dance in!

Get the Look

This photo of Jenny and the one below of Val and friends is the proof of just how popular maxi dresses were. Being long, and often flowing, they are forgiving for less than perfect figures--probably one of the reasons they were universally popular! Here's an example of a velvet 'peasant style' maxi dress with big bell sleeves. Jenny's bell sleeves on her bridesmaid dress show this shape off perfectly. You can see that the maxi dress really did come in many shapes and styles, so it may take a while to find the one that's right for you.

Here we have Helen in an early 70s burgundy number. We've created an outfit inspired by her's using a plum suede mini, matching shoes and a Georges de Feure, Art Nouveau print top. These prints were reproduced frequently on shirts, tees and dresses during the decade and were another display of the influences from the first half of the 20th century.

Last but not least we have Jane and Derek's wedding photo. Victoriana was another big influence in the 70s, as can be seen on Jane's wonderful high-neck bib dress, and on this handmade red, paisley maxi. This dress is also a great example of a 'leg o' mutton' sleeve, where a wide sleeve narrows from just below the elbow to the wrist, this is very flattering way to hide the 'bingo wings' and enhance a slender forearm!

ICONS

1970s Icon – Farrah Fawcett

Our 70s icon is Farrah Fawcett. Her relaxed style, casual glamour and flowing locks were the envy of all. Even in jeans and a t-shirt Farrah cuts a dash.

The key to most of Farrah's looks are a pair of high-waisted flares which are actually a pretty flattering look, as the flare balances out your hips. Jo's wearing an original pair of Brutus jeans, and a 70s checked, western shirt as sported by Farrah herself in some pictures. The shirt needs to be figure hugging and tucked in. We've accessorized with a stretchy gold belt to add a pit of glamour to an otherwise very casual outfit. The shoes are a pair of 90s high-platform clogs, which are a good go-to for recreating 70s shoes.

Farrah's trademark was her long, flicked hair, so with this look we had to use a wig. This is a modern, 70s style wig (it's the same one we've used for 'Bonnie and 'Marilyn', what value for money!) and really finishes this outfit. It signifies that this is meant to be Farrah Fawcett rather than just a generic 70s look.

Farrah was a natural 70s beach babe so eyebrows can be quite natural.

Choose bronzes, and golds to go with your shimmering tan, use a light colour all over the eyelid then highlight outer edge and socket with well blended darker shades, a bit of sparkle would be nice.

Plenty of mascara, no obvious eyeliner is necessary.

Use bronzer over a blusher, preferably with a bit of shimmer and fake the California tan!

A lick of of shimmering gloss in pink or coral over the lips.

1970s

119

Look Book / Daywear

Here's more 70s day fashions to inspire and delight. It was such an eclectic era that borrowed design ideas from other decades whilst making them its own.

Carpet cardigan coat.

All-in-one hot pants suit – hot pants were a uniquely 70s invention, a new daring extreme following on from the mini skirt!

Long suede waistcoat with multi-patterned shirt beneath.

Crochet belt.

Metal rose pendant.

Tooled tan leather clutch bag.

Blue floral 'granny dress' with bell sleeves.

Pink floral 'Prairie dress'.

Long polyester patterned maxi skirt.

Indian printed cotton, 'hippie' dress.

Brown suede belt.

Cheese cloth blouse, synonymous with 'hippie' fashion of the era.

Wide brimmed green felt hat.

Suede waistcoat with appliqué flower design.

Green wool coat with furry collar and cuffs.

Classic 70s outfit combining a polyester maxi dress with large collars, floppy hat, crocheted cardigan and a patchwork suede bag.

Small suede buckle satchel bag.

Cameo pendant and chain, part of the Victorian design revival.

Nylon floral blouse.

Early 70s lace-up boots.

Red leather-look handbag with bead detail.

Black velvet hat.

Gold flower brooch.

Yellow patterned head/neck scarf.

Green leather zip-up jacket, note the super wide collars here.

Harlequin pattern maxi skirt.

Aztec-style patterned midi dress.

Sheepskin hat.

Pink and blue shoes.

Black leather shoulder bag.

Embroidered cheese cloth top.

Quilted Indian cotton waistcoat.

Towelling turban, a 40s throwback.

1970s

Metal fish design souvenir bracelet.

Beaded headband.

Cream and checked linen suit.

Blue polyester jumpsuit, another 70s fashion favourite.

Pink patterned, Indian cotton ethnic dress.

Brown boxy handbag.

Purple wool coat with furry collar and cuffs

Look Book / Eveningwear

70s eveningwear had visible disco influences with lots of metallics and sparkle.

Silver bellbottom disco pants.

Silver lamé and orange polyester, disco midi dress.

Gold charm bracelet.

Burgundy clutch bag.

Purple crushed velvet jacket.

Green maxi dress with pleated caplet feature.

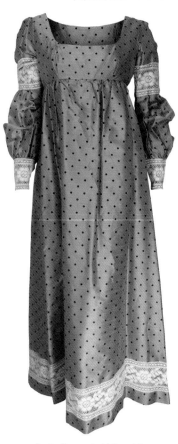

Spotted 'peasant-style' maxi dress.

Large beaded brooch.

Green velvet turban.

Grey slingback shoes.

Silver high heel disco sandals.

Purple spotted lamé, disco two-piece.

Floral, halter neck ruffled maxi.

Earth tone lamé maxi dress.

Gold plastic beads.

Gold boxy evening handbag.

1980s

The 1980s were a real contrast to the Hippie ethics of the 70s. The 80s said bye-bye to tie-dye and hello to power dressing professionals.

Thanks to the Women's Lib movement of the previous decades, business was booming for women. Women needed a strong silhouette to compete in a male dominated arena. The 40s offered inspiration in the form of sharp tailoring: large shoulder-padded blouses were worn with more 40s inspired flared or pencil skirts with court shoes. There were very masculine elements to this look, such as the tapered trouser suit, but also a sexy, glamourous side. TV shows like *dynasty* and personalities like Joan Collins encapsulated power dressing with added 'luxe' and became icons of the trend. The over-sizing seen in the 70s continued in the 80s but in different forms with big perms, big earrings, puffed sleeves and ruffles, all adding to a woman's presence in both work and social situations.

Eveningwear incorporated big, extravagant cocktail dresses, which could be off the shoulder, asymmetrical or sleeveless. The platform shoes of the previous decade were replaced with intimidating stilettos, more extreme than the 50s version.

At the opposite end of the fashion spectrum was a casual, sporty look. The sportswear phenomenon carried over from the late 70s was the 'play hard' flipside to the yuppie 'work hard' lifestyle. Gym class and dancewear such as leggings, leotards, ra-ra skirts, over-sized sweatshirts and legwarmers, became everyday street wear in the 80s. Tracksuits, formally a sports-only uniform, were adopted for general leisure and day attire. It was also the boom of trainers as a staple footwear for all. Films such as Fame and Flash Dance perpetuated this look and there was more interest in fitness and going to the gym, or at least looking the part!

Denim still dominated but was bleached or stone-washed, with straight or tapered, skinny legs for jeans, in contrast to the flares of the 70s. There was a huge nostalgia for the 50s and Levi's 501 jeans were a part of that revival. The interest in all things 50s was pretty much across the board, seen in film, TV and music. Icons of 50s fashion returned such as Rayban's Wayfarer glasses, leather jackets and cotton dresses with a full skirt, worn with ankle socks and pumps.

The 50s revival was probably also responsible for the somewhat saccharin side to 80s fashion. Pastel colours and florals were universal in tea-style dresses, with the trend epitomised by the British company Laura Ashley. When recreating 50s looks in the shop, 80s dresses can make the perfect substitute for original 50s dresses for enthusiasts and re-enactors, as the cuts and styles are very similar and they're half the price!

"LETS GET PHYSICAL"

Formal Daywear

This is a smart day look somewhere in-between Margaret Thatcher and Princess Di! After the 'anything goes' 70s, the flower children grew up and got jobs. Corporate fashion in the 80s was masculine, tailored and sharp. The 80s saw a return to the kind of matching accessories and hat wearing we saw in the 50s, with design elements from the 40s.

This is a double-breasted suit with 40s-type square, padded shoulders on the jacket and a pencil skirt. It's worn here with a pussy bow, paisley blouse and accessorised with a white handbag which would match the white stilettos, or could be worn with a blue shoulder bag to match the suit. We've picked out a classic 80s hat, worn for formal occasions such as weddings. Big clip-on earrings are the ultimate 80s accessory.

Without the hat it could be worn 9 to 5 in the office; with the hat it's more wedding worthy.

Casual Daywear

This casual look could be straight out of an 80s American teen movie, we're thinking the cooler, older sister perhaps? The t-shirt would be slightly over-sized, tucked in and pulled over the stretchy butterfly belt a little. The stone wash denim skirt is an 80s wardrobe staple. The black felt hat would be worn at the back of the head. We've added a grey suede, chain strap bag, black flat shoes with dainty bows which would be worn with ankle or wrinkled-down-to-ankle-length socks, and some Wayfarer-style shades. College cool or what?

Power Blouses

Blouses were very popular during this decade and came in many colours and patterns, from the stylish to the outlandish, usually in silk or polyester. They could be oversized to be worn over leggings, or fitted to be part of office attire. There was a strong 40s influence here as they usually all had shoulder pads to create that ultimate sharp shouldered effect. These blouses could be dressed up or down, for day or evening.

Eveningwear

80s eveningwear was varied, but there was usually a bit of razzle dazzle whatever the look. In the 80s ladies were as glamourous in trousers for an evening out as they would be in a skirt or dress. Here's a stylish evening look using silky tapered trousers with a high satin waistband. We've chosen an evening crossover power blouse, in gold lamé. We've accessorised with wonderfully big gold spiky earrings, a wide belt with gold leopard, decorative clasp, a patent clutch and black suede shoes with unusual gold bevelled heels.

Cocktail Dresses

Evenings out in the high-powered 80s conjure up a cacophony of cocktail dresses for us, so we felt we this selection deserved a double page of their own. As you can see here, cocktail dresses could be over the top with as many tiers, ruffles and gathers as could be fitted into one garment. Every girl at the party would be trying to out do each other in their ostentatious extravaganza of an outfit!

Get the Look

The 80s were the era we grew up in so we have first hand knowledge of the decade, and photographic evidence of our own fashion favourites and faux pas.

The casual sporty wear trend was at the opposite end of the fashion scale to power dressing. For young people printed sweatshirts were a firm favourite, as can be seen on Clare (in the middle looking grumpy!) and friends in the photo, and this ski-themed Dash jumper here.

Our friend Jo D was one of those cool older girls in the 80s, here she is showing off her James Dean t-shirt! The 80s saw the hey day of the t-shirt, and music or icon shirts were a great way of showing your allegiances. Here we have an original Madonna tee, many of this type of vintage band shirts have been reprinted and are easy to get hold of.

Espadrilles and Jelly shoes were the summer shoe of choice, and here are the Wayfarer-style shades cropping up again.

This is a classic Princess Di-style, Laura Ashley sailor dress, similar to the one modelled by Elaine. Laura Ashley dresses were huge in the 80s, they excelled at demure English style and revived several vintage fashion styles through their lines over the years, covering Victoriana up to the 50s.

Here's Jo in her favourite 80s outfit. Ra-ra skirts were all the rage at the time and fluorescent socks were a new trend. Wear one pink and one yellow for an even trendier 80s look! She's wearing a copycat 'Relax' t-shirt and, of course, the roller boots are optional.

1980s

Get the Look

Black, white and grey were popular colour choices in the 80s. We've taken inspiration from this family photo of a black and white striped dress and found a pussy bow, power blouse that's in a similar vein. Wear with a black pencil skirt for a smart day or evening look.

More printed tops, this time cartoon characters. Graphic designs and character prints were on all kinds of clothes and collectibles. Here's Clare in her white Disney tracksuit and Greg in a Snoopy sweatshirt. This trend was worn by all ages.

Here's Jo in a fabulous red 80s ensemble of her own creation! High-waisted cords, red blouse and matching beret, beads and pixie boots. Ankle length 'pixie boots' were a must for all ages in this decade. This pair of grey leather heeled ones will be more flattering on the leg.

Tracksuits were the ultimate in 80s leisure and lounge wear, following on from their move from sport to street fashion in the late 70s. Worn with sports socks and trainers, you could go straight from the court to the couch!.

The 80s are a great place to start to dip your toe into vintage as pieces can be cheap and easy to find. As it's recent history have a root about your family's lofts and wardrobes, you never know what might turn up.

ICONS

1980s Icon – Molly Ringwald from Pretty in Pink

John Hughes films are 80s classics and universally loved. Molly Ringwald became the ultimate 80s 'girl next door' thanks to her roles in his iconic films such as *The Breakfast Club* and *Sixteen Candles*.

We've chosen to recreate her book-ish *Pretty in Pink* outfit. Clare drew the short straw with this outfit as, although Mollie pulls it off, it's not particularly flattering or glamourous! What it is though, is an undeniably 80s ensemble.

For this look you need lots of pretty pastels and creams. Lacy collared or beaded blouses, followed by a waistcoat, embroidered or brocade if possible. The grey and pink skirt here is almost ankle length, and we've used gold court shoes. You could also wear ankle socks and pumps.

Even back then this looked almost vintage with the accessories she had: granny pearls and cameo brooches. We've used a similar hat to the one in the film and pinned two pink flowers to it and used a metallic bag.

There were overt elements of the 50s revival in this film too and we can't help but begrudge the fact that she cut up her friends lovely, pink spotty, 50s dress to make her monstrous 80s prom dress at the end!

Clare had to do very little to her curly ginger Mollie hair! The make up for this outfit is very subtle, with the main points being pink blusher and lipstick. Pretty in pink all round!

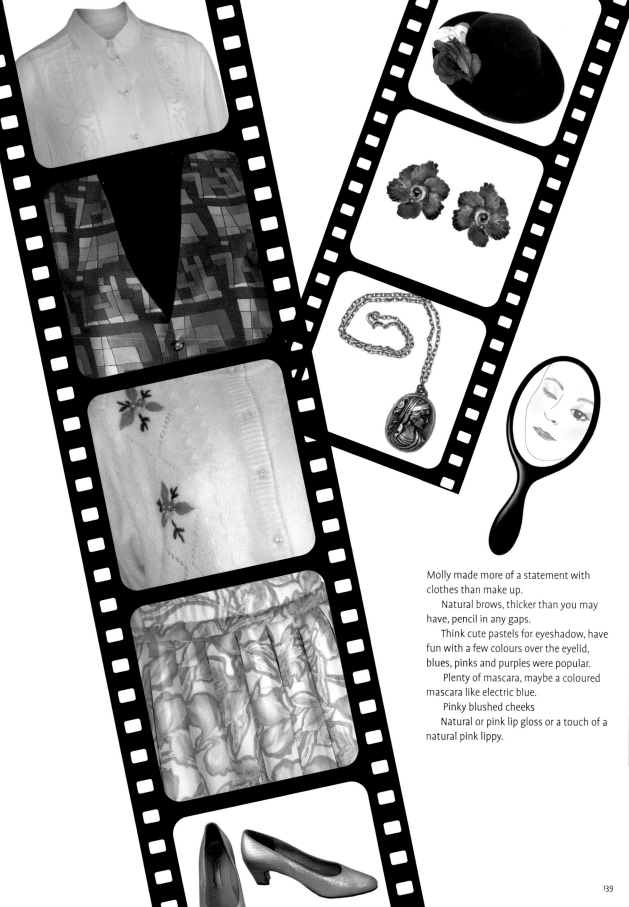

Molly made more of a statement with clothes than make up.

Natural brows, thicker than you may have, pencil in any gaps.

Think cute pastels for eyeshadow, have fun with a few colours over the eyelid, blues, pinks and purples were popular.

Plenty of mascara, maybe a coloured mascara like electric blue.

Pinky blushed cheeks

Natural or pink lip gloss or a touch of a natural pink lippy.

Look Book / Daywear

The 80s were a hotchpotch of design influences which we've touched on before, as demonstrated here with this eclectic mix of 80s daywear pieces.

Quirky instrument print bomber jacket.

Stone wash denim shorts with American flag pocket detail.

Bamboo print jumpsuit.

Black felt wide brim hat.

Brown peep-toe court shoe.

Gold leaf brooch.

Spotty wrap dress.

White elastic enamel rose belt.

Gold sunglasses.

Floral 40s style tea dress.

Faux fur coat.

Grey and hot pink leather clutch.

Batwing stripe silk top.

Big gold clip-on earrings.

Black occasion hat with feathers and net.

Tan leather buckle shoe.

Gold and pearl heart brooch.

Large straw sunhat.

Spotty t-shirt.

Peach checked sundress.

Brown leather shoulder bag

Polkadot wrap shirt dress.

Look Book / Daywear

On this page we've included more sporty
and youth orientated fashion

White and gold stiletto ankle boots.

Black and florescent baseball cap.

Denim jacket with Madonna
t-shirt underneath.

Leather belt with gold clasp.

Classic Jelly Bag.

Blue polyester jumpsuit.

Rose print, tiered cotton dress.

Pink floral visor.

Big red leather belt.

Green felt hat.

Purple plastic sunglasses.

Adidas tracksuit top.

Leotard and neon leggings.

Red Converse boots.

Stone wash, fringed and studded denim skirt.

Elastic butterfly belt.

Look Book / Eveningwear

The ostentatious 80s wasn't shy when it came to evening wear. Often more was more in the 80s, the more ruffles, the more glitz and glamour, the better.

Over-sized flower earrings.

Shimmery evening blazer.

Red leather clutch.

Silver shoulder bag.

Sequined cocktail dress.

Pink strapless drop waist dress.

Denim stilettos.

Black taffeta cocktail dress, with lace gloves and a black, gold and pearl necklace.

Laura Ashley cotton floral 50s-style gown.

Patterned stockings.

Black and leopard print double-breasted blazer.

Silver lamé double-breasted blouse.

Roses brooch.

Blue sparkly ruched dress.

Pink ruffle gown.

Black and lamé blouse.

Black peep-toe shoes.

Silver chain bag.

Red Chinese-style dress.

Wearing vintage clothing is as popular as ever, so much so that contemporary fashion companies are even making new clothes look 'vintage'. We don't think you can beat genuine vintage though, for its uniqueness, quality and its place in fashion history.

A lot of vintage pieces were much better made than today's equivalent. With our modern, disposable culture, what vintage fashion relics will we be leaving for future generations?

The majority of people that we come into contact with who buy vintage on a regular basis, are looking for unusual one-off pieces to add to their existing wardrobe. These might be pieces that are currently 'on trend' or classic design items that will never be unfashionable, or a quirky item that will make them stand out in a crowd. This approach isn't for the vintage purest, as it's about having fun with fashion, mixing and matching and creating a unique personal style.

By collecting classic vintage pieces, things that take your fancy from across the decades, for instance a classic looking 50s wicker handbag, a chunky 80s hand knitted cardigan, a tweed jacket or 60s shift dress, you can integrate these into your everyday attire, creating a distinctive, vintage-inspired style that's also timeless.

We asked vintage lovers to send in photos of themselves wearing and enjoying their vintage fashion. We've had a real mix of responses from people: from those who wear full, head-to-toe vintage on a daily basis and are immersed in a particular era, to those who like to mix vintage with modern. Where we've found people who love a particular decade we've asked them a bit more about themselves. We also kept our camera on us at all times when at vintage events as Second Hand Rose and took some snaps of stylish vintage fashionistas!

Take inspiration from the following pages and see how everyday, vintage is worn, whether as a full ensemble or blended with contemporary fashion, from designer to high street, for unique looks that are all the wearer's own.

Now you've learnt the rules that define fashion for each decade, you can break those rules by mixing vintage with modern clothing. Create your own look using fashion history as your inspiration!

Vintage Street Fashion

Alison Tang
Lady of the Parlour, London, UK

I am wearing one of my all time favourite vintage pieces. I purchased it online which I rarely do for vintage as you can never quite tell the quality and fabric. However it looked so beautiful and such a one of a kind find I went for it! It turned out to be a genuine piece made in Hawaii, 1950s and features lovely flutter sleeves with a gorgeous pattern on the fabric. I love full length dresses and it was just perfection. I hope to keep this to pass on one day.

My wardrobe is over flowing with vintage, repro, designer, High Street and made to measure pieces. Day to day I wear mostly 1940s, 50s or rockabilly inspired outfits. I like to be very glamorous when I am out and about so will occasionally opt for a more 1920s or 30s feel. I am never without my feline flicks and red lipstick. Most importantly, always style over fashion!

From the tops of my victory rolls to the soles of my platform heels I love the 1940s and 50s over all other eras. I love the femininity of the way women dressed, even during the times of war. Not being afraid to show your curves and using them to their full advantage! It really was the time when every effect made was appreciated.

Nothing perks you up and make you stand tall than when you have your hair coiffed and your red lips on. It's really important for me to feel good inside and out. And when you are feeling particularly down it's always best to paint on a brave face, just like the good ol' days.

http://dressingparlour.blogspot.com
Photo Credit: Kate Bloomfield:
http://katebloomfield.blogspot.com

Andi B. Goode
Adelaide, Australia

The dress I'm wearing in this picture is from the 1940s and I bought it from Etsy.com - I love the white eyelet details contrasting with the denim blue. The shoes are also from Etsy and date from the 1950s, I believe. The accessories are from various places and are new, vintage and some gifts!

For my personal style I like the 1940s and 1950s best but I do love fashion from so many different eras, though it is the 20th century in its entirety that captures my fascination the most in fashion history. I couldn't pin-point when exactly I fell in love with vintage clothes - I love the structure of them, the little details, the texture of the fabrics, the prints, the cuts...I even like the slightly musty smell so many of them retain! And favourites - sometimes I feel like asking asking a vintage lover to pick a favourite piece is like asking to pick a favourite child! Well, maybe not quite so difficult. I have this absolutely gorgeous green, burnt orange and white plaid dress which has four buttons near the neck and pockets on the hips. My favourite things in dresses are plaid, buttons and pockets and this combines all three!

There are so many people whose style I admire but one lady I always go back to is Dolly Parton and, in fact, many ladies of country music! I admire the fact that she has never compromised her personal vision of her style and I admire her big hair/wigs even more!

www.andibgoode.com

Catherine Regan
Photographer, Worcester

My love of vintage dresses began as a student in the eighties. I used to raid Oxfam shops for beautiful 50s dresses which I teamed with doctor martin boots. I still love scouring the charity shops and vintage shops for a unique look. For me it's all about the dress whatever era. I love 40s, 50s and 70s style. Good prints, well crafted, feminine and classy. I think my look still stems from those indie days, I've just included more modern pieces into my look to bring it up to date and it's become more grown up. Style influences have always been Grace Kelly, Audrey Hepburn, Sophia Loren and Beatrice Dalle.

cat1regan.blogspot.com

Jennifer Burton
West Midlands
Of RoyalTea
Vintage mobile pop up tea room

One of the reasons I love vintage clothes is the excitement in finding a unique garment and it fitting perfectly. It can be like searching for hidden treasure AND striking gold (and it's addictive!)

I love the fabrics and quality you get with vintage, something you wouldn't find with clothes from Primark. Vintage just seems to fit me far better than 'modern' clothes.

With my style I am aspiring to be Barbara by day and Margot by night! (From the BBC's 1970s TV show The Good life)

I don't think I have a favourite era, I do love the 70's but that could just be my Good Life obsession! I also love the lines and fabrics from 50's & 60's. But I don't say no to fantastic 80's Kaftans either!

Photos By Catherine Regan Photography - cat1regan.blogspot.com

Chloe Morton
Kidderminster, United Kingdom

I love the 80s: the fashion, the music and the cars; each a complete work of pure splendour. I would describe my style as 'Twenty-First century New Romantic".

Sadly, when most people think about the 80s they imagine neon leg warmers and big hair but look deeper and you find that the decade was actually a thing of beauty. My interest in 80s style lies mainly within the New Romantic movement which in itself looked especially ostentatious and effortlessly glamorous. The frilly shirts and bright make-up may have seemed exaggerated but that is what I admire, the non-conformity, the confidence to turn their back on the mainstream and make a statement.

The music is just as striking to me; synthesisers were now in a league in their own, adding to the musical complexity and quality that I feel songs today lack. My heart rate still quickens during the crescendo of Ultravox's 'Vienna' and I still get goosebumps every time I hear Nick Rhodes' opening synthesisers in Duran Duran's 'Save A Prayer. When you can still get physiological reactions like those to songs you have listened to hundreds of times you know you have found something special. It was the stuff of magic and I believe over time people have forgotten its magnificence.

My interest in the 80s began when I was about 12 years old. It all started when I heard *You Spin Me Round (Like A Record)* by Dead or Alive and I instantly adored the song, it wasn't until I heard *Vienna* by Ultravox and *Planet Earth* by Duran Duran that I realised that my affection for the decade had grown from a penchant to unbridled passion. The music from this decade now dominates my music collection as does the fashion within my wardrobe. The style side of things really blossomed a few years ago when a vintage store opened in my local town and 80s vintage finally became accessible to me. It started with one off pieces but as I became ever more enamoured with the decade I was making more and more purchases and it now makes up a large section of my wardrobe! I hope that one day it will fill my garage too as a continuing dream of mine is to own a scarlet red 1983 Audi Quattro! A motor I have adored for many years.

Nick Rhodes, the founding member and keyboardist of Duran Duran is my fashion icon of the 80s. After all, Duran Duran were called 'the pretty boys of pop' for a reason! Most people are surprised by this because they imagine female 80s fashion role models to be someone like Madonna or Cyndi Lauper, so when I say my style has been mainly influenced by a gentleman they seem quite shocked! But that is another joy of 80s fashion, particularly New Romanticism; it was a very androgynous time so gender played no large part in style. Take for example the power suit, if anything women looked more masculine then men, they probably wore less make up too! For me Nick's fashion, no matter what the occasion, never fails to look anything less than perfect, even today. He makes bold fashion choices that no other person would dare to make and pulls them off flawlessly, I really admire him for that. It is this which has given me the confidence to say that I am fully contented with my vintage style and have no plans to conform to today's fashion. I am stuck in the 80s and I couldn't be more proud!

(above) Classic 80s vintage New Romantic frilly blouse.
Black Skinny Jeans.
Gold weave belt.
Gold snake skin effect court shoe heels.
(inset) 80s Vintage blue bat winged knitwear jumper with sequin peacock detailing.
Black Skinny Jeans.
Navy blue leather belt with gold detailing.
Black bow suede peep toe court heels.
Photographer: Emily Silk.

Coralie Ruiz
France

Coralie works in House of Vintage in London. She likes to mix vintage and designer and mix items from different decades. She's wearing a Preen sweater, vintage dress and customised loafers from eBay: she's added vintage posies to them.

www.houseofvintagelondon.blogspot.com

Dagmara — Vintage Girl
Lodz, Poland

I love vintage clothes, accessories and jewellery. It's a window into past, beautiful and elegant eras. The time when clothes were made of good quality fabric, well finished, with excellent details. I like to wear vintage clothes because it gives me a pure pleasure and brings me closer to previous decades. From my collection I really love soft and very stylish leather gloves from my grandmother, a turquiose dress from Paris and green woolen suit from 50s.

I have many style icons, I love all the girls I've come to know through their blogs: vixenvintage. blogspot.com, caseyselegantmusing.blogspot.com, freelancerfashion.blogspot.com and many other girls from all over the world.

From the past I adore all those beauties from the 40's and 50's like Rita Hayworth, Marilyn Monroe, Hedy Lamarr, Ava Gardner, Lauren Bacall, Veronica Lake, Betty Grable; I love their feminine style, class and the inspiration that they give me every day.

www.vintagegirl.blox.pl

Amy Jensen
AKA Dizzy Dame
Midwest, USA

In this picture I'm wearing a 1940s dress. I love the print and the colors. I wore a handmade snood with bakelite bracelets, the shoes are remix vintage. I wore this outfit to a hangar dance and won 'Best Dressed'. My favorite era for fashion is the 1930s, there is nothing like the glamour of the past! It's not a costume for me, it's my everyday thing.

www.thedizzydame.blogspot.com

Eleanor Coole-Green
Kidderminster, England

My style changes day to day, vintage one day, tramp the next

Fran Horne
Malvern

When I'm shopping for clothes I tend to look out
for genuine Victorian and Edwardian items, but
also slightly more modern 60's and 70's 'Victoriana'
reproductions. I also buy militiaria relating to WWI
especially anything with a scientific or medical
theme. I'm keen on pocket watches, old chains and
vintage leather items. I'm not a typical steampunk in
that I don't wear or buy goggles! But I do very much
like vintage hats and accessories relating mainly to
the Victorian era. I buy a fair number of damaged
vintage jewellery and linen which I make into new
items.

www.ixykix.com

Street style

Georgina Lander
Worcester, England

I've been dressing in 40s clothes full time for about 3 years now but have been collecting related all sorts since I was sixteen, so it's been 5 years in all. There isn't one thing I particularly love about the 40s: it's the design, music, the social history and of course the fashion. I'm fascinated at how there was still a want / need to look your best and fashionable through times of danger and uncertainty. With restrictions on practically everything people had to make the most of the old and find nifty ways of making new. Also the time put into doing this. Who nowadays would take the time or even bother to re-knit a jumper or re-fashion one of your fella's suits into a sporting little number for yourself?

Originally I started collecting costume jewellery, but this soon branched out into clothing and accessories and now I collect anything that appeals to me from the 20s through to the 50s, focusing mainly on the 30s and 40s. This includes packaging, magazines, knitting and sewing patterns, furniture, kitchen / homeware and wartime memorabilia.

It's hard to chose a favourite from my collection but firstly I would have to say my Evacuees. They are life size child mannequins from the 1950s (or earlier) called Edmund Arthur Askey, Trudy May Trinder and Baby Peggy Lee. At the moment they are all dressed in a mix of original 40s and homemade clothes that Ma and I have made for them. Secondly my green Tala meat safe filled to the brim with my beloved knitting pattern collection. And lastly an outfit made up of an early 40s green woollen suit with an military air, a late 30s / early 40s brown straw tilt hat (my very first tilt) a white pair of utility peep toe platforms, and last but not least my favourite pair of white 1930s sunglasses: I love them to bits but unfortunately one day I'm sure they will end up in bits!

As for 40s fashion, I like Schiaparelli's designs. Also without sounding too cheesy, just every day people and relatives from the era. For me their photos are the best resource and inspiration one could have.

http://ticketybootupney.blogspot.com

Jack Parrott
London

Jack loves vintage shirts and is working on a his collection of Hawaiian shirts. Here he's wearing a vintage short-sleeve shirt and carrying a vintage holdall.

Jamie-Rae

I saw that you need some vintage lovers for your book, I have attached a few photos

I have always loved vintage clothes, as a kid I used to dress up in my mum's American thrift shop dresses, many of which are now in my wardrobe and then a few years ago I inherited a mother lode of dresses, skirts, tops and fabric from a friend of the family. Dressing up makes every day feel a bit more special, I just wish I had the balls to wear a hat every day and not just on special occasions

Jill MacLachlan
1920s/30s Enthusiast
Ontario, Canada

I love the 20s and 30s because of how beautiful and original many of the garment designs and fabrics were. I also love how much of the clothing reflects the spirits of these eras: for example, the looser, uncorseted silhouettes and higher hemlines of many later 1920s dresses reflect the fact that this was a time when many women were really pushing past many old gender norms.

I love late 20s and 30s sportswear and resortwear, perhaps because these types of garments reflect an energetic and modern spirit of travel and adventure that seemed to prevail during this period, and perhaps because many pieces were designed with both movement and elegant glamour in mind. Of course, I don't only love the fancier clothing worn by the leisured classes during these periods. I am as entranced by a humble little dustbowl feedsack dress as I am by any dazzling silk charmeuse evening gown. I definitely think my love of Thirties feedsack dresses stems from the connection I feel to memories of my grandparents' stories of the hardships they endured living on the Canadian Prairies during the Great Depression.

I also love 30s knitwear, perhaps because each piece stands as a testament to the industriousness of the depression-era home-knitter, who, despite financial restrictions, created such awe-inspiring handmade artistry. One way or another, I love how various garments from the 20s and 30s capture important histories of the people who lived through these time periods. Whenever I wear a piece of vintage, I feel connected to those histories.

It's so hard for me to pin down one, favourite icon from these eras. I do love Jean Harlow. She looked just as fantastic in casual wear as her famous "painted on" gowns. I'm also a big fan of Myrna Loy. Her wardrobe in the first Thin Man gets me every time I re-watch it, and off screen, she seemed like she knew how to put together an outfit. While she was an incredibly controversial figure, I must concede that Wallis Simpson was a chic-er than chic style icon as well.

Perhaps due to the relative scarcity of intact, wearable clothing from these eras, 20s and 30s clothing can be very pricey. However, it's not impossible to find some real treasures at bargain prices. The key is to be persistent and patient. I often find 30s clothing is so misunderstood by even experienced vintage sellers. As a result, you'll often find 30s garments mislabelled as being from the Victorian period or the 1940s; as a result, on occasion, you can find some fiendishly underpriced, but fabulous deco frocks. To really get these deals, you need to educate yourself about the fabrics, silhouettes, and design elements that really define typical garments from this era. That way, you'll be able to pounce when you see a deal! You also can't be a perfectionist if you are a vintage bargain hunter in love with the 20s or 30s. Mint condition items from this era can go for sky high prices. If you know how to sew or are some who finds little age spots and beauty marks on clothing "endearing," you can again snag some great deals on some amazingly unique and beautiful garments.

I think accessories are often more affordable to collect, especially if you're starting out. Depression-era ladies on a budget knew how to create amazing looks with very basic rayon dresses, simply by changing up their hats, gloves, purses, and scarves. You can get some beautiful little carved celluloid bracelets or earrings for very reasonable prices. I personally adore many of the inexpensive but fun little matching cuff and collar sets you'll find floating around. These were also used by industrious deco ladies on a budget to add variety and character to otherwise simple black, brown, or navy dresses, so they can be a great way to spice up one's own modern vintage wardrobe.

My first photo depicts my visit to the Fashion History Museum in Cambridge, Ontario and I'm wearing a 1930s black and white floral print rayon dress and my favourite 30s/40s off-white heels.

The second photo captures a magical night of dancing to big band music at Casa Loma in Toronto. I'm wearing a 1930s pale blue bias cut evening gown with matching flutter sleeve capelet jacket and vintage inspired peeptoe satin shoes.

www.
lettersfromhomefront.
blogspot.com
www.adelinesattic.etsy.
com

Karen Tunnel
Worcester, UK

I like to mix vintage and modern to create a unique look. There's something about the 70s that particularly appeals to me and that I'm drawn back to time and again.

Karina
Japan/London

Karina is from Japan and loves 40s and 50s fashion, in particular the style of Rita Hayworth.

In this photo she's wearing an Agnes B Shirt (she works for Agnes B), Hey Day Vintage Trousers, and second hand shoes.

www.karinatanabejones.com

Katie MacKay
London

Every morning I feel like a wee girl with a dressing-up box; picking and choosing pieces to create a look that's full of pattern and colour. With those being my wardrobe must-haves, vintage wins hands down every time - especially when I'm looking for a unique, striking print. But beyond the garments and accessories themselves, I love to imagine what story each vintage piece could tell. I like the romantic notion that they've all lived a little.

http://www.whatkatiewore.com

Lucille Needles
Nottingham

My vintage style is: flirty, feminine and floral. Everything must be high waisted, preferably authentic and I'm a sucker for making sure my whole entire outfit is colour co-ordinated (even down to my underwear!!)

My favourite pieces are a pair of polka dot pedal pushers (the comfiest things to just slip on and look fabulous) and a beautiful dress with layers of netting decorated with hundred of little pink flowers. I bought it from Baltimore, it cost me too much money and I still haven't worn it yet, but it hangs on my wall and just looks pretty!

My Vintage idols are Betty Grable, Diana Dors and Carmen Miranda. They were the sexiest women around, without even trying too hard!

My top tip for creating the perfect hairdo is as follows; back comb, pin securely and spray, spray, spray the hell out of it, if there are any mistakes, just stick a pretty flower of the top!

callmelucille.blogspot.com

Pod and family
Quinton, Birmingham

We had the pleasure of visiting Pod's home, meeting her lovely family and seeing her impressive wardrobe collection first hand. It was like stepping back in time. All her clothing and accessories are neatly filed away, with a whole new wardrobe of 60s clothing for each year. Pod won't wear the same dress again to do's and events, and labels them after an outing so she knows exactly where and when they're worn so they won't be duplicated. It's fascinating to see!

It all started I suppose listening to my mom and dads records, The Who, The Kinks and The Monkees. I remember stacking up the record player with the singles and singing along over and over again, happy days!

Then it was the late 70s, I'd already seen a few scooters around and thought how cool they looked. One of them was owned by a lad I'd grown up with so I knew him quite well and got chatting. The style was amazing and he was talking about the groups I'd been listening to all those years ago. I was at the age when you needed to 'belong' and this fashion seemed the natural way for me. I started going to 'mod' discos where another friend DJ'd, then it was endless. Life soon revolved around dancing, records and hunting down clothes in charity shops.

Then a certain film was released called Quadrophenia! A crowd of us went to the local cinema to see it. It was like a revelation, like someone had got inside my head and could see how I felt. And as they say, along with all the other mods, it spoke to us and it soon became 'a way of life'.

And here we are, 30 years later and still as excited about the whole scene. I have a wonderful husband who thankfully understood my passion and slipped into the whole 60s thing like a duck to water, and a daughter who grew up knowing nothing else. Life's so easy when you're in household that everyone can relate to each other and talk about the same music and fashion.

I feel very privileged wearing the clothes every day and giving them another lease of life. They aren't just another item of clothing, they already have a history of their own and deserve to be respected. After all, they have lasted this long and still look good.

The 1960s was an era of style, so different from today's fashion of showing your pants!! Where did it all go wrong? There was naivety and innocence but also freedom. This reflected in the fashion and music. Just think of some of the icons from that decade and how they have influenced the pop stars and fashion designers of today. Now that's something you can't argue with!

Robert Darch
Photographer and filmmaker
Exeter

In these photos I'm wearing a 1930s Alexandre Savile Row Tailored Suit. The photos were taken at Fagins Antiques, Devon. (www.faginsantiques.com)

I like that vintage clothing is more often than not unique. My suit is pushing 80 years old, yet it's in a beautiful condtion. It has outlived owners, and seen its way through a World War. I love that it carries a history that will never be known. The High Street is now a pretty dull and uniform place to shop with all the chains following each other like sheep: it's purely about commerce.

They need to make money, so they convince people that they have to buy a new wardrobe every six months. Fashion is now on the whole designed to be consumed & then thrown away. I doubt that anything you buy nowadays will make it past a decade, let alone nearly a century.

www.robertdarch.com

Photo credit: Ben Borley, photographer.
www.benjaminjborley.tumblr.com

Sammy Davis
New York City

I love vintage because I believe that these pieces of clothing remain with us for a reason. They are representative of energy that has a positive place in this world, just waiting for the right girl or guy to be attracted to its energy and as I like to say, "give it a happy home."

When you've fallen in love with a piece of vintage, you've fallen in love with something much deeper and meaningful - yourself. Dressing in vintage is pushing your creative boundaries. It inspires our full potential. When we can wear vintage, and love ourselves in those pieces, we feel inspired! And inspiration is the driving force of happiness. Therefore, it all links back: Vintage inspires fashion happiness!

I'm currently lusting my 30s bias cut silk slip dress, floral palazzo pants from the 60s and suede leather skirts from the 80s in turquoise and sienna. I love finding vintage pieces that speak to today's trends, and then styling them to truly represent who I am and aspire to be.

I wish I could be Jimi Hendrix on stage in full costume, just for one show! And then there is always my fantasy to shop the vintage closet of Madonna, or my other vintage blonde icons: Debbie Harry and Stevie Nicks. We can't forget Bianca Jagger's amazing style a la Studio 54, and the "I am woman hear me roar" fashion fix of Diana Ross!

There are so many amazing vintage boutiques in New York City. I love nothing more than stepping into a store and feeling the aura of those treasures and also the personal style of the owner who has curated the store according to his or her tastes. I wear vintage not just for great style, but great support of small business owners. So when shopping vintage I do everything I can to buy from the boutiques who fuel the economy of a local community.

I would describe my own style as 'Modern girl with a vintage fashion twist'.

http://www.sammydvintage.com &
http://www.youtube.com/sammydavisvintage

Solanah Hernandez
AKA Vixen Vintage
Northwest USA

I'm wearing all clothing from the 1950s: flannel lined jeans, handmade cropped sweater, Pendleton 59er jacket, novelty socks, red wingtip shoes, and a red bandanna.

I love this outfit because it's something I turn to on chilly Northwest days. A lot of people think to wear vintage, you have to always be dressed to the nines, in heels, and hats, and restrictive undergarments. While those are all wonderful, I love the casual looks that our grandmothers, and great grandmothers lived in day to day. Especially handmade things, like this sweater, and this jacket was made from fabric produced at a local mill. Casual, vintage, and local, doesn't get much better than that!

www.vixenvintage.blogspot.com

Sydney Ballesteros (Syd Divine)
Arizona, USA

The appreciation for vintage clothing and style has been such a big part of my life, for as long as I can remember. My mother and grandmother were both very stylish ladies in each of their era's and own right. It has always given me the opportunity to express my creativity and love of putting things together. I really began experimenting with vintage clothing heavy in high school, mostly because I had my own job and would get my pay cheques on Fridays, then hunt for treasures at the local thrift stores and yard sales on the weekends. This was a crucial age for me to be different and innovative. I have an undying love for many eras of vintage clothing. It is important for me to find the beauty and inspiration in many things, and never miss out on anything. I find something special and intriguing about fashion all the way back from the 1500's to the glamour of the 30s, and onto the free spirits of the 1970s. When I started collecting vintage clothing, the eras I was mostly drawn to, were the 1940s & 50s. I still deeply love these decades in fashion, but it is always evolving.

Honestly, I have too many "favourite things" in my collection, that is my problem-ha!ha!ha!

I am automatically attracted to a polished chic-ness in style, so not to sound cliche, but right off the bat, I am drawn to Grace Kelly, Audrey Hepburn and Jacqueline Kennedy, but there are so many women from each decade that I look to for inspiration. It is so hard to narrow it down!

www.goldengirlofthewest.blogspot.com
Photos by: Susana Victoria Clark
Vestigepinup.com

Ulrika
Helsinki, Finland

I am a Burlesque artist called Cherry Dee Licious a.k.a. Turrrbo Cherry. I perform in a group called The Itty Bitty Tease Cabaret and we also give classes.

I mostly wear vintage because of the loom and style of it. Like many others, my favorite eras are 1920s to the 1960s, but the past years I've been mostly fond of the late fifties and early sixties. I like to wear vintage from that time because the cut and shape of the clothing suits my body and my sense of aesthetics. Vintage has of course an ecological aspect too, but as long as I keep on buying online from abroad I can't really say I'd go for vintage for any eco friendly reasons. I do also wear vintage inspired, repro or retro. For me, it does not really make that much of a difference whether I'm wearing vintage or just vintage inspired, the overall look and feel is the most important for me.

When buying vintage I try to choose items that are of cotton or another well breathing material, I do not feel comfortable in thick polyester for example. Before I used to get all dolled up on a daily basis, nowadays, on basic weekdays, I aim for a more calm everyday timeless style: sort of fifties casual. I am especially fond of shirtwaist dresses and cropped pants. When I think of vintage in general I mostly think of clothing, but I do in fact have a lot of vintage accessories too; most of my bags are vintage. I just don't think that much about it.

(right)
The jacket is in fact not vintage but new. My shoes, the beret and the necklace are vintage however. It describes my way of wearing vintage quite well, mixing old and new. The shoes are my grandmother's from the early fifties.

(right)
is what I feel I look like a lot nowadays. The knitted sweater and trousers are my grandmother's. About half of my vintage is from both of my grandmothers and their sisters.

(left)
I'm wearing a 1950's cotton dress. I love old day dresses, as they nowadays work for both more and less formal occasions depending on how you style them. This is one of my favorite dresses and the one I wore when my husband proposed.

www.freelancersfashion.blogspot.com

Lizze Marx
London

No one person inspires Lizzie's eclectic style: "just things that catch my eye, often things from the 40s and 50s."

Lizzie also is drawn to patterns, textures and silks. She is wearing a vintage dress from New York (Fabulous Fanny's) and has Peruvian worry doll style earrings to match the people-shaped tassles on her dress.

Esther & Jake Redfern
Birmingham

Brother and sister Jake and Esther Redfern are both interested in vintage fashion. Jake is currently inspired by the 1920s for fashion and everything. Esther lives in London and mixes vintage with a modern edge.

Antonia Miejluk
Morecombe, UK

I love the 40s and 50s, the music, dancing and the effort people put into their outfits.

www.blackout2.com

Deborah
London

I manage a vintage shop and I'm inspired by 40s Hollywood film stars

Hannah and Sean O'Kelly
Surrey

We love the 40s in particular, and are really getting into the 40s way of life, I've even handmade this hat.

Neil Donoghue and Kathy Hanson
Leicester, UK

We love dancing and have a passion for Twentieth Century history

Victoria Blackburn-Harris, Worcester, UK

This is a photoshoot I did for my friend's art project. The dress is an amazing 70s, dip-dye Grecian-style maxi dress.

ReeRee Rockette, London
Owner of Rockalily Lipstick

I am wearing a vintage dress (I call it my dinner lady dress!) with a vintage petticoat underneath and a cheap high-street belt to cinch in the waist. I am wearing vintage glasses and Rockalily Rockette Red Lipstick.

I love vintage and vintage style clothing as it makes me have fun with fashion. It's a little like playing dress up each day! Why would I wear boring clothes when I don't have to!?

www.rockalily.com

Vintage at Southbank

These stylish people were snapped at Vintage at
Southbank 2011 - www.vintagebyhemingway.co.uk

Harriet Parry
Midlands, UK

My main inspiration comes from the 1920s
and primary colours

Eve Styliamides
Birmingham

I like unusual things from every era.

Jo and Julie

We love 40s America, especially the music and dancing.

Josyane Bijoux
London

I take care of the vintage items I have but I enjoy them and wear them. I love being glamourous and mixing things up with modern.

John and Cinzia
London

This is us dressed as usual, our every day look.

Phoebe
Singapore

I just love vintage and anything old!

Louise Nimmick and Claire Powell
Hockley, UK

We love getting dressed up for special occasions.

Vix Brearley
Walsall, UK

For me the seventies epitomizes freedom, sexual equality, liberation and individualism; The Isle of Wight festival and travelling overland on the Magic Bus to India. The Rolling Stones' album Exile On Main Street and the subsequent film following Mick, Keith and the gang during their 1971 self-imposed tax exile in the South of France, summed up seventies perfection to me, hedonism, hippiedom and effortless glamour.

Although the entire decade was fabulous, embracing everything from punk, disco, metal and glam rock, it was the early 1970's that really stood out for me: hot pants, lace-up boots, tooled leather, ethnic-inspired kaftans and silver jewellery brought back from India, maxi dresses, floppy hats, Crimplene, flares and platform soles.

I was born in 1966 and became aware of 1970s fashion as a child dragged around Bus Stop, Van Allan, Biba and Richard Shops by my fashionable mother. The vibrant patterns, extravagant designs and flamboyancy of the clothes Mum picked out were exciting and summed up the heady mystique of adulthood. Many a time I'd sneak out of bed to observe her entertaining her friends at home over a Cinzano and lemonade, dressed in a Jean Varon maxi or a Bus Stop satin cocktail dress. I adored dressing up in her clothes and couldn't wait to reach an age when I was old enough to buy my own.

From an early age I adored glamour and preferred to spend my pocket money on antique satin kimonos from Oxfam and armfuls of chintzy 1950's frocks from jumble sales rather than dolls and games. As a skinny teen I found the shapes of the 1970s dresses, the empire-line cut, halter necks and A-line skirts suited my slender frame most. 1970s fashion is still something many vintage fashion enthusiasts despise and consequently pickings are rich. I frequently find fabulous dresses on eBay for less than £5 and my local charity shops will save anything "loud, mad and bright" especially for me. My weekends are spent scouring jumble sales, flea markets and car boots for vintage clothing, accessories or fabric for me to cut up and make my own from dressmaking patterns I've found on my travels.

I have many icons from the 1970s: Bianca Jagger, Anita Pallenberg, Cher, Parveen Babi and Helen (both Bollywood stars) to name but a few. I only have to Google their names if I'm feeling uninspired and I find hundreds of fabulously inspiring images.

www.vintagevixon.blogspot.com/

Clare

In these photos I am wearing a mix of vintage Chanel, Gucci, YSL and Chloe with other vintage finds from London, Worcester and online. I particularly like vintage pieces from the 1930s and 40s as well as the 70s. I get inspiration from films such as Almost Famous, Gosford Park and Boogie Nights. I'm also inspired by muscians such as Prince and Michael Jackson. I love the thrill of finding a beautiful silk dress that's almost 100 years old that fits me perfectly: it feels more special than buying it from a regular shop. My favoyrite pieces are my vintage Chanel bags- they would be the first thing I grabbed if my house was on fire!

Oliver

Fashion has always been a big part of my life and my family have been a major influence in my love for fashion. From birth my mother dressed me in head-to-toe designer outfits and my Nan is the most fashion conscious person in my family, and at 91 still buys me amazing items. Christmas Day at my house is like London Fashion Week, only with more booze, more food and everyone has a Black Country accent.

I was brought up to know how to dress for every occasion. One MUST dress to fly, dress for the theatre and dress for a Sunday. Making an effort with what I wear makes me feel alive. Fashion is my therapy.

When I was 16 I was given my father's old sheepskin coat from the 1970s, it had no buttons and the sleeves were too short but I loved it and ten years on I still wear it every winter. That coat ignited my love for vintage.

In these pictures I'm wearing a variety of vintage clothing which I have collected over the years from many different places including Barcelona, Birmingham, Brighton, London, Marrakech, Paris, Worcester and many more. Whatever town, city or country I'm in, I always go on the hunt for a vintage bargain.

If you were to ask me what my favourite decade is for style, I couldn't give you just one. I love the fashion from the 1950s, 1960s and 1970s and I am influenced by magazines, books and websites. I don't believe in having 'a style' or 'a look' because in this day and age there is a time and place for every era.

Acknowledgements

Many thanks to the talented photographer and graphic designer Matt Walford, who worked his magic on the majority of images in this book. (www.mattwalford.co.uk)

Several of the items we've included from the 20s to the 40s were from the collection at Worcestershire County Museum at Hartlebury Castle. Many thanks to Anita Blythe at Hartlebury for all her help and enthusiasm. Thanks also to Sarah Bourne at The Commandery Museum Worcester. (www.museumsworcestershire.org.uk)

We borrowed several pieces from Plastic Fish Costume Hire. Many thanks to Aeileish Watts. (www.plasticfishcostumes.com)

We also want to thank: Jane and Georgina Lander for lending us some fabulous 30s and 40s treasures to photograph. Loll Newman from Toadstool Vintage (www.toadstoolvintage.com). Rocket Originals for images of their fantastic reproduction vintage clothing. (www.rocketoriginals.co.uk). Dead Men's Spex for the images of their vintage spectacles. (www.deadmensspex.com). ReeRee Rockette of Rockalily Lipstick. (www.rockalily.com)

Thanks also to: Val & Tony Bolton, Careen Bourke, Chris Bourke, Doreen Bourke, Helen and Chris Bridge, Jo & Greg Dunn, Shaun Hencher and the Hencher family, Jenny Hull, Jane & Derek Walford, Pam & Pete Waterhouse, Verna Webb, Dawn Weston and Betty Wolf. Thanks again to all who contributed their photographs for the vintage street fashion section, please take the time and check out their blogs and webpages. Last but not least thanks to Lee Ripley and all at Vivays Publishing.

Other handy links to websites or products we've mentioned along way:

www.whatkatiedid.com
www.pendleton-usa.com
www.freddiesofpinewood.co.uk
www.remixvintageshoes.com
www.heydayonline.co.uk
www.lauraashley.co.uk
www.horrocksesfashions.co.uk

Jo's and Clare's websites:
www.secondhandroseworcester.co.uk
www.facebook.com/secondhandroseworcester}
www.jowaterhouse.blogspot.com
www.concretetocanvas.co.uk
www.worcestervintage.blogspot.com